OUR KNOWLEDGE OF THE INTERNAL
WORLD

Lines of Thought

Short philosophical books

General editors: Peter Ludlow and Scott Sturgeon
Published in association with the Aristotelian Society

OUR KNOWLEDGE OF THE INTERNAL WORLD

ROBERT C. STALNAKER

CLARENDON PRESS · OXFORD

OXFORD

UNIVERSITY PRESS

Great Clarendon Street, Oxford OX2 6DP

Oxford University Press is a department of the University of Oxford.
It furthers the University's objective of excellence in research, scholarship,
and education by publishing worldwide in

Oxford New York

Auckland Cape Town Dar es Salaam Hong Kong Karachi
Kuala Lumpur Madrid Melbourne Mexico City Nairobi
New Delhi Shanghai Taipei Toronto

With offices in

Argentina Austria Brazil Chile Czech Republic France Greece
Guatemala Hungary Italy Japan Poland Portugal Singapore
South Korea Switzerland Thailand Turkey Ukraine Vietnam

Oxford is a registered trademark of Oxford University Press
in the UK and in certain other countries

Published in the United States
by Oxford University Press Inc., New York

© Robert C. Stalnaker 2008

British Library Cataloguing in Publication Data

Data available

Library of Congress Cataloging in Publication Data

Data available

Typeset by Laserwords Private Limited, Chennai, India
Printed in Great Britain
on acid-free paper by
Biddles Ltd., King's Lynn, Norfolk

ISBN 978-0-19-954599-5

1 3 5 7 9 10 8 6 4 2

Contents

Acknowledgements

The ideas developed in this book first took shape, in overly compressed form, in the Whitehead Lectures, given in the spring of 2004 at Harvard University. I am grateful to the Philosophy Department at Harvard for that opportunity. The invitation to give the John Locke lectures at the University of Oxford in the spring of 2007 gave me the stimulus to develop the ideas in more detail, and I thank the philosophers at Oxford, both for the invitation, and for their hospitality during my term there. I was fortunate to give these lectures at a time when philosophy at Oxford is particularly lively, and I benefited from discussion both with the faculty and with an excellent group of graduate students, including Brian Ball, Michael Blome-Tillmann, John Hawthorne, Maria Lasonen-Aarnia, Ofra Magidor, Daniel Morgan, Simon Saunders, Nick Shea, Ralph Wedgwood, and Tim Williamson.

Philosophy at MIT is also particularly lively these days, and we too are blessed with excellent graduate students whose comments and questions have helped me to sharpen and clarify my ideas and arguments. Discussion and correspondence with Rachael Briggs, Sarah Moss, Dilip Ninan and Seth Yalcin about self-locating attitudes were particularly helpful. Suggestions from Robert Fogelin, Agustin Rayo and Scott Sturgeon each helped me to see things I had missed, and led to what I hope are improvements.

My colleague Alex Byrne read a draft of the entire manuscript and gave me incisive comments on every chapter that were extremely helpful in the final revision.

Thanks, once again, to my editor, Peter Momtchiloff for his advice and support. It is a pleasure to work with him, and with the staff at Oxford Univesity Press.

Finally, thanks to Heather Logue for suggestions and corrections at the last stage of the editorial process, and for preparing the index.

Cambridge, MA
December 2007

I

Starting in the Middle

Analyze theory-building how we will, we all must start in
the middle.

W. V. Quine[1]

The Cartesian picture of the mind, and of the world, was under
attack from a variety of directions throughout most of the last
century. We were taught to do without private objects, and private
languages, the myth of the given, the ghost in the machine, the
Cartesian theater, things present to the mind. We became materi-
alists, or at least functionalists. We naturalized our epistemology: instead of trying to build a foundation from the materials we
found in our internal worlds, we were advised to start in the middle
of things, to observe how people in fact went about justifying
their beliefs, and to explain their knowledge in terms of the way
they interact with the things in the world that we, as theorists,
find there. But the Cartesian beast is a hydra-headed creature that
refuses to be slain, and that continues to color our philosophical
pictures and projects. Wittgenstein, Ryle, Quine, Sellars, Davidson
(not to mention Heidegger) may have cut off a few Cartesian
heads, but they keep growing back. Descartes is not the bogeyman

---

[1] Quine (1960), 4.

he once was; Cartesian skeptical arguments, and arguments for the autonomy of minds and mental states are back in fashion, and philosophers feel free again to observe and contemplate the inner objects that Wittgenstein tried to banish.

The Cartesian target is of course a broad and diverse one: critics of one aspect of the picture may embrace another, and anti-Cartesians sometimes accuse each other of being closet Cartesians. (There is a cryptic and jarring remark in one of Donald Davidson's late papers about naturalized epistemology: "I do not accept Quine's account of the nature of knowledge, which is essentially first person and Cartesian."[2])

Being myself still mired in the philosophical mindset of the twentieth century, my discussion of our knowledge of the internal world will be in the anti-Cartesian tradition. My subject matter will be that part of our knowledge that the Cartesian internalist takes to be most basic and unproblematic—knowledge of our own phenomenal experience and thought. But I will approach the subjective point of view from the outside. Before getting down to work on the details, I will try, in this first chapter, to set the context by making some "big picture" remarks about the way I see the contrast between a Cartesian philosophical project and an externalist alternative. I will sketch some old themes that are familiar in themselves, but that are not always recognized as playing a role in the details of some of the current debates that I will be discussing.

The contrast I have in mind is a contrast between two kinds of philosophical project, rather than two different metaphysical theses—a contrast between decisions about where to start, between different assumptions about what is unproblematic, and about how to characterize the central philosophical problems. The Cartesian internalist begins with the contents of his mind—with what he finds by introspecting and reflecting. This is what is unproblematic;

---

[2] Davidson (1991), 192.

these are the things and the facts that we know directly. The internalist's problem then is, how do we move beyond these to form a conception of an external world, and how are we able to know that the world beyond us answers to the conceptions that we form. The externalist, in contrast, proposes that we begin with the world we find ourselves in, and with what either common sense or our best scientific theories tell us about it. Among the things we find are human beings—ourselves—who are things that (it seems) can know about the world, can experience it, have a point of view on it. Our problem is to explain how our objective conception of the world can be a conception of a world that contains things like us who are able to think about and experience it in the way that we do.

The contrasting projects will formulate the central philosophical problems about knowledge and the mind in quite different ways. For the internalist, the central question about intentionality, for example, is this: how can my representational capacities extend beyond my own mental life? I can take for granted, without explanation, my capacity to represent the contents of my mind, and my capacity to reason about what I find there. At this point, there is no problem about the relation between my thought and its subject matter, since they are identical. The problem is to explain how I extend my representational reach beyond this. So the problem is a problem of explaining representational resources for a wider domain in terms of given representational resources for a narrower one. The problem is like the problem of explaining the logical and semantic relation between an observation language and a theoretical language. The externalist sees the problem of intentionality quite differently: we find in the world human beings, with a certain complex physical structure, a certain range of behavioral capacities and causal relations with their environments. What is it about those features, capacities and relations that makes it correct to describe the internal states and verbal behavior of these creatures in terms of intentional relations to propositions, properties, and individuals? What is it for such complex physical objects to be in states that are *about* the world, and about themselves?

Internalists and externalists will each complain that the other is taking for granted what needs to be explained. The internalists see the externalist project as a project motivated by pessimism. Their complaint is this: "Because you see no hope of reasoning your way out of your internal world, you give up and simply *assume* that there is a world that answers to your inner conception. You just help yourself to some additional material, taking it for granted because you see no other way to make progress. You decide that honest toil is so ill paid that theft is the only option." But the externalists reject this way of understanding their project. "It is not," they insist, "that we are taking for granted what you take as given, and more besides. It is you, we think, who are taking for granted phenomena that are in need of explanation. In our view, we can make sense of your starting point—the internal world—only by locating it in a wider world. The problem, we think, is not that skepticism is unanswerable, from a purely internal point of view, even though it may be true that it is. (In fact, we argue that the problem of skepticism, seen this way, is worse than you think.) The problem is rather that skepticism about the external world has as one of its sources an uncritical acceptance, and a false conception, of our knowledge of the internal world."

As will be clear, my sympathies are with the externalist in this debate, but my main concern will be to keep clearly in mind what perspective it is that we are taking. Problems about knowledge and the mind have usually been posed, in recent times, in a way that presupposes the externalist starting point, but Cartesian and traditional empiricist ideas that presuppose an internalist perspective continue to influence the way we think about those problems, and some of the puzzles about our knowledge of our own experience and thought may arise from equivocating between internal and external perspectives. To try to make the contrast between the two approaches clearer, I will discuss briefly four examples of places in recent and current philosophical debates where I think a shift from internal to external perspectives has played a crucial role. I will start with a look back at Hume's problem of induction, and what he calls his skeptical solution to it. Second, I will look at a discussion by Wilfrid Sellars of contrasting ways we think about the relationship between the qualitative character of visual experience and the properties of things in the world that such experience helps us to detect. Third, I will look at the debates between direct reference theorists and descriptivists, and related debates about anti-individualism, in Tyler Burge's sense of that term. Fourth, I will review what David Lewis called Putnam's paradox, and the response to it that he, following Michael Devitt, defends. Each of the examples deserves much more discussion than I will give them here. My aim at this point is just to highlight some recurrent themes that I see in these familiar examples, themes I will explore in more detail in later chapters.

While internalists and externalists begin at different points, and formulate the central problems in different ways, both are aiming to provide a conception of the world as it is in itself. After sketching the four examples, I will conclude this chapter by considering what Bernard Williams says about how this aim should be understood.

1. SKEPTICAL SOLUTIONS TO SKEPTICAL DOUBTS

The classic example of a shift from an internal to an external perspective is Hume's skeptical solution to his skeptical doubts about induction. The problem of induction is first posed from the perspective of the subject: the problem is how to justify the inferences one makes from one's evidence to hypotheses about the external world, and about the future, where the available evidence is restricted to "the present testimony of our senses and the records of our memory."[3] The shift (once it is established that the problem, posed in this way, is insoluble) is to view the subjects who are in this predicament as objects in the world who are making inferences about it, and to ask how they do it, why they do it as they do, and why it is that they are as successful as they are. The skeptical solution offers a psychological theory that provides a descriptive account of the conceptual resources that these creatures (ourselves) use to form beliefs, and a causal explanation of how they acquire and use those resources. But the story is not just a descriptive one: we observe not just that these creatures are disposed to behave in certain ways, but that they have a *capacity* to find their way about, reliably, in their environment, and our external theory provides an explanation for that capacity, an explanation for the fact that the methods of inference that they use to form beliefs are reliable methods. Of course the proponent of the skeptical solution is using the very methods that he is assessing in arriving at the conclusion that the world is one that is conducive to the success of those methods, but to acknowledge this is just to acknowledge that the skeptical solution is not a solution to the skeptical problem on the internalist's terms. The explanation for the reliability of the inferential methods used by these creatures is still a substantive one, and it is not a foregone conclusion that the procedure will result in a positive assessment. What is required is that the story the externalist tells from the middle of things, about what the world is like, be one that is in harmony with the hypothesis that he is a creature who is able to tell this story and to have good reason to believe that it is true. Even this requirement may seem to be out of reach, if one mixes the internal and external perspectives in an inappropriate way. So, for example, suppose one took the Humean external story, and the skeptical solution, to be something like this:

---

[3] Hume (1748/1977), 16.

X (the defender of the skeptical solution): "There is really no such thing as causation, so the world is like a random sequence of states, but it is a sequence that happens (by sheer chance) to have exhibited, up to now, a certain pattern of regularity, *and it will continue to do so* (still by fortuitous coincidence) so we can be confident that our inductive methods will continue to work."

S (the internalist skeptic): "But what reason do you have to be confident that the pattern will continue?"

X: "I can't give you a reason, but I can give you an explanation for my confidence. I am a creature of habit, and the regularity of the pattern up to now has irresistibly caused me to expect it to continue. I can't help having this belief, and it is a good thing too, since the pattern *will* continue."

One might, with good reason, find X's line here to be not just unsatisfying, but incoherent, since he purports to be giving a causal explanation for a certain belief, while rejecting the applicability of causal concepts. But the real Humean does not reject causation, and emphatically affirms the central role of causal hypotheses in inductive reasoning. What is rejected is only a certain theory of causation that (according to the Humean diagnosis) tries to explain a relation between events in terms of a relation (necessary connection) that applies only to ideas. The Humean also will reject the conclusion that we can have reason, grounded only in what is available from the internal perspective, to believe any causal claims. So much the worse for the internal perspective.[4]

[4] *I* say "so much the worse for the internal perspective", but I can't claim that Hume says this. He remains, I think, profoundly ambivalent, taking his skepticism as seriously as his naturalism. There is some suggestion that he thinks it is a weakness that we (and he) are unable to stick consistently with the unmitigated skepticism that he argues for, but also a suggestion that it is a good thing that we are weak in this way.

I will leave it to the Hume scholars, who have long argued about the tensions between the naturalist and skeptical strains in Hume's thought, to determine whether there is a stable position, faithful to the texts, that reconciles these two strains. But whether there is or not, I think it is clear that Hume's skeptical solution makes the kind of externalist shift that I am trying to illustrate. (Thanks to Robert Fogelin for helpful discussions about Hume's skepticism, and his so-called skeptical solution.)

2. VISIBLE PROPERTIES AND VISUAL EXPERIENCE

On the traditional empiricist picture, ideas of visible properties—of color properties, for example—derive from visual experience, which is then in one way or another projected onto the world. This picture can be developed in various ways, and is compatible with very different theoretical accounts of the nature of the properties that we are detecting, or at least take ourselves to be detecting, when we have visual experiences. On one view, color is a confused concept that involves attributing to things in the world properties that are really properties of our experience; on another, color is a power or a disposition to cause us to have experiences with a certain character, a power that resides in the physical objects to which we ascribe color properties; on a third view, colors are whatever the categorical properties are, the possession of which by an object in a perceiver's vicinity tend to cause her to have experiences with a certain phenomenal character. What these ways of developing the empiricist picture have in common is the assumption that our concepts of color properties are derivative from concepts of certain types of phenomenal experience.[5] On a contrasting externalist view, as developed for example by Wilfrid Sellars,[6] the ascribers of color properties begin with a naive view of an objective world, with things in it to which our most basic color concepts are applied. We don't, to begin with, have a theory about how we are able to determine the colors of things, or about the nature of the color properties that we can see that things

[5] The contrasting views of the nature of the color properties themselves are not tied to this empiricist thesis about the conceptual priority of a concept of color experience. One might, for example, combine a physicalist, or even a dispositionalist view of color properties with the thesis that our concepts of colors as properties of things in the world are prior to our concepts of the experiences that those properties tend to cause in us.

[6] Sellars (1956/1997).

have; we just learn how to tell that things are red or green, blue or yellow, and the ability that we acquire constitutes our possession of the concepts that we are applying. When we become more critical and self-conscious about the nature of our capacities to detect these properties, and of the limitations of those capacities, we theorize that our ability is explained by the fact that we are sometimes in certain internal states that tend to correlate with the presence of the property detected, and we also learn that the correlation is not perfect. As a result, we come to distinguish *being* red from merely *looking* red. The new, more sophisticated concept of looking (to one) to be red (or of there looking to be something red before one) applies when one is in the hypothesized internal state, even when the normal correlation fails to hold. On this Sellarsian, externalist picture, it is the objective properties, or our concepts of them, that have *conceptual* priority; the idea that we can be in internal states corresponding to the colors of things, and our concepts of the qualitative character of those internal states, derive from a quasi-theoretical hypothesis about our relation to those properties of visible things. But while our concepts of the qualities of our experience are derivative, the qualities themselves have a kind of *explanatory* priority: they play an essential role in the explanation of our capacity to detect, by looking, the colors of things, and an essential role in the causal explanation for our acquisition of the concepts that we are applying when we detect color properties. The internalist's mistake, according to the Sellarsian diagnosis, is to conflate the two kinds of priority, and this conflation distorts the epistemic role that something like sense contents play in our perceptual knowledge.

Quine makes the same distinction, and paints a similar picture, most explicitly in the introductory chapter of *Word and Object*. "There is every reason to inquire into the sensory or stimulatory background of ordinary talk of physical things. The mistake comes only in seeking an implicit sub-basement of conceptualization, or of language . . . . Our ordinary language of physical things is about as basic as language gets."[7]

The issues about priority that Sellars discussed remain controversial. They are complicated, not only by different ways of spelling out the relevant notions of priority, but also by different views about the nature of the relevant experiential properties. Christopher Peacocke for example, defends the apparently anti-Sellarsian thesis that experiential concepts are *definitionally* prior to our concepts of the colors of things in the world.[8] But he also disclaims a commitment to the consequence that possession of color concepts requires possession of a concept of experience. "All this experientialist requires for the possession of the concept of redness is a certain pattern of sensitivity in the subject's judgements to the occurrence of red' experiences" (where "red'" ascribes the relevant experiential property).[9] This sounds like a causal, rather than a definitional dependence, and it might be a commitment that Sellars would have accepted. But Peacocke's priority thesis, as I understand it, does have the consequence that one whose normal way of detecting the property *red* was by having an experience with a different qualitative character (as in the notorious inverted spectrum case) would thereby have a different concept of the property. In this sense, the concept essentially involves a certain type of experience, according to Peacocke's priority thesis.

But what exactly is this experiential property, *red'*? According to *intentionalists* or *representationists*, the phenomenal character of experience is to be explained in terms of the intentional content of experience—the way an experience represents things to be.[10] Peacocke's priority thesis is tied to a rejection of intentionalism, and the assumption that experiences have an intrinsic qualitative

---

[7] Quine (1960), 3.   [8] Peacocke (1984).   [9] Ibid., 59.
[10] Intentionalism can be spelled out in different ways. For a defense of one of them, see Byrne (2001). 'Representationism' is Ned Block's term. He characterizes and criticizes it in Block (2003).

character that is prior to any representational role that experience may play.[11]

The externalist story, as told by Sellars and Quine, does not imply that the qualitative properties of experience are representational properties, but it does imply that our conceptions of those properties are derivative from their representational role. First comes the naive capacity to detect, and then a proto-theoretical account of representation (not a general account of what it is to represent, but just a recognition of a difference between the way things are and the way they seem to be, and a recognition of a difference between something represented and something in oneself that is doing the representing). The theorist of the mind hypothesizes that there are these internal properties—qualia—that explain our capacity for visual detection. So according to this story, our recognition of qualia derives from our recognition that we are representing in a particular way.

3. DESCRIPTIVISM AND THE CAUSAL THEORY OF REFERENCE

The received view of reference that Saul Kripke criticized in *Naming and Necessity* has its origins in an internalist picture of representation, and even though at least some of the post-Kripkean neo-descriptivists would disclaim any allegiance to a Cartesian project, I think that intuitions from that project play a role in motivating defenses of this account of reference, and that it is useful to see the parallel between the Kripkean critique and the kind of externalist project promoted by Sellars and Quine.

Reference to individual concrete things, such as human beings, is particularly problematic, from an internalist point of view, since

---

[11] Though Peacocke explains the primed properties such as *red'* as properties of a visual field, and I would have thought that a visual field is a feature of an essentially representational mental structure.

such objects are paradigm cases of things that are not denizens of the internal world, and so not things to which we might have direct access from the inside. The descriptivist strategy is to explain the capacity to refer to concrete individuals in terms of a capacity to refer to the properties and relations that are exemplified by such individuals, things that might more plausibly be thought of as internal to the mind, or at least as things that the mind could grasp from the inside. Of course Frege was clear that the contents of thought are not themselves mental objects—they are something more abstract that can be objects of the thoughts of different thinkers—but he still seems to have assumed that the contents of speech and thought must be, in some sense, internal to the mind. Frege was famously incredulous at the idea that physical objects like Mt. Blanc (with all its snowfields) might be constituents of a proposition. Russell disagreed, holding to the view that propositions might indeed have physical objects as components. But in the end Russell took the bite out of this externalist doctrine by combining it with the view that propositions could be grasped only by someone who was *acquainted* with all of their constituents, where acquaintance required the kind of perfect and complete knowledge that we could have only of mental objects or of universals. There are propositions with Mt. Blanc as a component, and we can describe such propositions, but they cannot be the contents of what we are saying or thinking when we talk or think about Mt. Blanc. So while Frege and Russell had different conceptions of a proposition, if we restrict ourselves to propositions that are candidates for the contents of speech and thought, then both of these founding fathers of the received view of reference will agree that singular reference to physical objects must be mediated by general concepts that apply to those objects.

Kripke's externalist critique begins with arguments against the descriptive adequacy of the descriptivist project: in some cases that seem, intuitively, to be examples of successful reference, the speakers lack the conceptual resources that the analysis requires them to have; in other cases, it was argued that the analysis implied the intuitively wrong conclusion about what the referent is. A second part of the critique argues that even if a descriptive analysis were correct, it could not provide a satisfactory account of reference without an explanation of how we are able to refer to, or to express, the properties and relations that are expressed in the descriptions that constitute the analysis. What is questioned here is the internalist presupposition that our intentional relations to properties and relations are unproblematic. A descriptivist analysis just passes the buck from one kind of expression to another. This point was supported by the arguments that Tyler Burge gave against what he called individualism. If general terms, along with names and other singular referring expressions, depend for their semantic values on environmental conditions, then our intentional relations to them cannot have the kind of foundational status that the internalist project requires. Speakers and thinkers cannot have the kind of "perfect and complete" acquaintance with properties and relations that is necessary (according to the internalist) to grasp the propositions expressed in the descriptivist analyses, and so further reduction is required for the success of the internalist project. Here it is important that the anti-individualist arguments apply to a wide range of general concepts—not just to a few natural kind terms and theory-laden scientific terms, but even to purely qualitative predicates. If only a relatively narrow range of terms and concepts are "twin-earthable" (to use David Chalmers's term), then there might be a prospect of a reduction of the concepts that are in this narrow range to those that are not. But the externalist argues that the phenomenon brought out by the anti-individualist thought experiments is ubiquitous. There is no foundation. We need an explanation of another kind.

At this point, the externalist makes a distinction that parallels the distinction made by Quine and Sellars between conceptual and explanatory priority. Singular reference with a proper name is *conceptually* direct, but that should not be taken to imply that there is no explanatory story to be told about what it is in virtue of which a name refers. Just as it is a mistake to confuse explanatory with conceptual priority in the case of visible properties and visual experience, so it is a mistake (according the causal theorist of reference) to confuse an explanation for the fact that a name refers as it does with a conceptual analysis of what is expressed by that name. A definite description of an individual named might play an essential role in the explanation for the fact that the name refers to that individual even if the propositions expressed with the name are determined as a function of the individual itself, and not of some concept expressed by the description. Kripke took Frege's notion of sense to involve an equivocation between these two roles of a descriptive concept in the explanation of the relation between a name and its referent.[12]

Despite the influential critique by Kripke and others, the descriptivist program remains alive. "Description theories of reference are supposed to have been well and truly refuted," David Lewis wrote in 1984. "I think not: we have learned enough from our attackers to withstand their attacks."[13] Lewis was sensitive to the distinction between a conceptual or semantic role for a description and an explanatory, or metasemantic role, and he acknowledged that a causal descriptivist analysis—one that builds the description of the causal process by which the reference of a term is determined into the semantics for the term—just passes the buck to the terms used in the description. He nevertheless argued that such an analysis was defensible, and preferable to an account that located the causal story in the external account of the facts in virtue of which thought and talk has the content that it has.

---

[12] Kripke (1972), 59: "Frege should be criticized for using the term 'sense' in two senses. For he takes the sense of a designator to be its meaning; and he also takes it to be the way its referent is determined. Identifying the two, he supposes that both are given by definite descriptions."
[13] Lewis (1984), 60.

Even though Lewis wanted to defend what is, in a sense, an internalist project, he accepted the externalist's formulation of the problem of intentionality, and he argued that any solution to it will require a move that, I will suggest in the next section, parallels the move in Hume's skeptical solution to the problem of induction.

4. PUTNAM'S PARADOX AND ITS SKEPTICAL SOLUTION

Lewis's externalist shift, like Hume's, is a response to a skeptical problem that is posed from the subject's point of view. The problem is what Lewis calls Putnam's paradox, an argument that Hilary Putnam posed first in 1977.[14] The rough idea is this: Start with the fact that any consistent theory has many interpretations according to which it is true. All that needs to be assumed for this result is that there are enough things in the world; nothing need be assumed about what those things are like. But actual theorists claim more than that their theories are true on some interpretation or other: they *intend* a certain interpretation, and the claim is that the theory propounded is true on that interpretation. What Putnam's skeptical argument challenges is the assumption that this provides any constraint at all on interpretation. For I might formulate my referential intentions (in my public language, or in my language of thought), and add them to my total theory, and the resulting augmented theory, incorporating statements expressing all of my referential intentions, will still be true on many interpretations, no matter what the world is like. The point applies quite generally: suppose that there is some condition C that we might propose as a constraint on admissible interpretations of our language (or on whatever the objects or events are that represent our thoughts). C itself could be incorporated into one's theory, and

[14] Putnam (1977).

the argument applied to the resulting theory. "Constraint C is to be imposed by accepting C-theory, according to Putnam. But C-theory is just more theory, more grist for the mill, and more theory will go the way of all theory."[15] The point is that all that any such constraints can do is to restrict the range of consistent theories that are candidates to represent a subject's corpus of beliefs. But since any such theory will be true, on many interpretations, the restrictions do not help to constrain the content of the claim that the theory makes about the world.

But Lewis replies: "C is *not* to be imposed just by accepting C-theory. That is a misunderstanding of what C is. The constraint is *not* that an intended interpretation must somehow make our account of C come out true. The constraint is that an intended interpretation must confirm to C itself."[16] The constraint is imposed, not on oneself from within, but on the objects we find in the world, who are in fact ourselves.

Like Hume's skeptical solution, this response to Putnam's paradox does not answer the internalist skeptic on his own terms. The conclusion of Putnam's argument is that all reference is radically indeterminate, and Lewis's strategy can succeed in stating a determinate condition only if this conclusion is false, so the response might be thought to beg the question. Lewis does not take this worry very seriously: who gave the skeptic the license to set the terms of the debate? But he takes more seriously what he describes as "a deeper and better reason to say that any proposed constraint is just more theory."[17] He thinks that it is tempting to believe, of whatever theory of reference is correct, that "somehow, implicitly or explicitly, individually or collectively, we have made this theory of reference true by stipulation." And he thinks that if this tempting belief were accepted, Putnam's conclusion would be unavoidable. "The main lesson of Putnam's Paradox," Lewis

[15] Lewis (1984), 62.
[16] Ibid. See also Devitt (1983), which Lewis cites in this context.
[17] Ibid., 63.

writes, "is that this purely voluntaristic view of reference leads to disaster." But I think this is a misleading diagnosis. We don't need Putnam's paradox to see that any general solution to the problem of intentionality that tried to be purely voluntaristic would be incoherent. An intention is an intentional state, and a stipulation is an intentional act whose content is determined by the content of the intention with which it is performed. One obviously cannot explain what makes an intention that is directed at Osama bin Laden be an intention that is directed at *him* in terms of the agent's intention that it should be directed at him. A purely voluntaristic theory of reference makes sense only as a theory that aims to explain *linguistic* intentionality in terms of the intentionality of thought, and a project of this kind (Grice's project, for example) is untouched by Putnam's paradox. I think the main lesson of Putnam's argument should instead be put this way: a formulation of the problem of intentionality as a problem for the subject of the intentional states ("how should *I* establish a connection between my thoughts and what they are to be about") is hopeless. A clear view of the problem requires that we distinguish, conceptually, between (1) ourselves as theorists attempting to explain our intentional relations to things in our environment and (2) ourselves as the objects whose relations to things in their environments we are studying. But as in the case of Hume's skeptical solution, our two views of ourselves must be in harmony: a satisfactory account must explain how it is possible for us, as objects in the world, to be the kind of thing that can have a theory of the kind that we, as theorists, have, and it must explain how such theories can succeed in saying things about the world.[18]

Each of these four examples involves a dialectical shift from the subject's perspective to the perspective of a theorist. A problem is formulated, or reformulated, as a problem about the relations

[18] Putnam's paradox is often compared with the skeptical puzzle about rule following that is posed by Kripke's Wittgenstein. And Kripke does refer to Wittgenstein's solution as a "skeptical solution". See Kripke (1982).

between beings found in the world who are only accidentally the same as the ones who are posing the problem. The questions are not, how should *we* justify our inductive practices, or bring it about that our thoughts extend beyond our minds, or that our words attach to things in the world, but how are *their* capacities to learn about the world, or to talk or think about it, to be explained, where *they* are of particular interest because they happen to be us. But since they *are* us, the shift, in each case, raises potential problems about circularity. Responding to these problems requires distinguishing between different kinds of priority, and imposes a demand that the theorists' explanations of the cognitive and epistemic capacities of their objects of study be in harmony with the fact that they themselves are able to give the kind of explanation that they are giving.

5. THE ABSOLUTE CONCEPTION OF REALITY

It is tempting to think of this external standpoint as a view of reality from outside, or from above. We retreat into our objective selves, leaving behind our empirical selves, and take on the view from nowhere.[19] This image is reinforced by the language of perspective: the external standpoint seems to be a perspectiveless perspective. But in a way this image gets things exactly backward. It is essential to the view from the middle of things that there is no place from which to observe and reflect on the world other than our place within it. It is essential that the theorist viewing himself as an object in the world is the same as the object being viewed. It is not that we are looking for a platform outside of the world on which to build our conception of it; instead, we are trying to do without foundations at all.

[19] Cf. Nagel (1986).

Both internalists and externalists are aiming at a conception of a reality that exists independently of our conception and knowledge of it. They differ about whether such a conception can be built from within, and perhaps also about what such a conception requires. Bernard Williams, who was concerned with Descartes's project of generating such a conception, suggested that there is something puzzling and problematic about an absolute conception of reality. Here is the problem, as he saw it:

Suppose A and B each claim to have some knowledge of the world. Each has some beliefs and moreover has experiences of the world, and ways of conceptualizing it, which have given rise to those beliefs and are expressed in them: let us call all of this together his *representation* of the world (or part of the world). Now . . . A's and B's representations may well differ. If what they both have is knowledge, then it seems to follow that there must be some coherent way of understanding why those representations differ, and how they are related to one another.

We need, that is, to understand how the different representations "can each be perspectives on the same reality." This requires one

to form a conception of the world which *contains* A and B and their representations; . . . but this will still itself be a representation, involving its own beliefs, conceptualizations, perceptual experiences and assumptions about the laws of nature. If this is knowledge, then we must be able to form the conception, once more, of how this would be related to some other representation which might, equally, claim to be knowledge; indeed, we must be able to form that conception with regard to *every* other representation which might make that claim.

But the idea that there might be such a conception, Williams goes on to argue, poses a dilemma:

On the one hand, the absolute conception might be regarded as entirely empty, specified only as 'whatever it is that these representations represent'. In this case, it no longer does the work that was expected of it . . . . On the other hand, we may have some determinate picture of what the world is like independent of any knowledge or representation in thought; but then that is open to the reflection, once more, that that is only one particular representation of it, our own, and that we have no independent point of leverage for raising this into the absolute representation of reality.[20]

The first step in defusing this dilemma is to distinguish the content of a representation both from the particular means used to express that conception, and from the act of expressing it. The absoluteness we are looking for is in the content: we want a representation of the world as it is in itself (or as Williams puts it, "of what is there *anyway*") and not just of the world as it appears from a certain perspective. But of course any representation of the world as it is in itself will use certain means to say that the world is that way, and the saying of it will take place at a certain time and place in the world.

Suppose I am A, forming a conception of the world as it is in itself. It is part of the content of my conception that there are conceivers forming conceptions of the world (as it is in itself), and that those conceptions are formed from a particular point of view within the world. If my conception is correct and reasonably inclusive, then among those conceivers will be someone who is me (A), and someone else who is B. My account will recognize that A and B are conceiving of the world from different perspectives, and will include an account of how those perspectives differ. But since the particular conceptions being formed by A and B that we are interested in are conceptions of the world as it is in itself, it will not be part of the *content* of A's conception that it is A who is forming that conception (though it will be part of A's conception that A is, at a certain time and place, forming *a* conception with that content). It could be that A and B form exactly the same conception of the world as it is in itself. In this case, there will be distinct acts of conceiving, each a conception formed from a certain point of view, but they will have the same content.

[20] Williams (1978), 49, 50.

Now, as Williams suggests, it may be that the conceptions of A and B are *not* the same, in either form or content, even if both are correct (both count as knowledge), and the two conceptions may differ even if both are correct representations of the world as it is in itself. Each may tell only a part of the story, or they may, as Williams suggests, tell the story in different but equivalent ways.

Some things Williams says suggest that the absolute conception he is looking for must be *comprehensive*, incorporating all possible representations of the world. It is not entirely clear what this would mean, and I don't think that a conception of the world as it is in itself requires that completeness is achievable, or even intelligible, but suppose we can make sense of the idea. Consider a possible world that contains a representation of itself that says enough so that anything else that might be said would be redundant. There is, in this world, a book (with very small print) in A's library. Since the book is complete, it will tell us that there is a book on the shelf of A's library that tells the complete story, and it must also tell us exactly what the book says. One might be tempted to imagine an infinite regress here, like a picture of a room that has a picture of the room on the wall, and so of smaller and smaller pictures nested within one another. But self-representation need not require this regress. It is easy for a book to tell us, among other things, what the book itself says. At the appropriate point, the book might say: "On the third shelf of A's library, there is a book that contains the following text: (now turn to the top of page 1 of *this* book, and read through to the end; then return to this point, to finish the story of what else there is in the world)". Is this a cheat? Does A's book really give us the complete story? Well, imagine a description of this possible universe that is not in the universe at all. A's world is, after all, a mere counterfactual possibility. Suppose *we* have a complete description of A's counterfactual world. Our book is just like the book in A's library, except that at the appropriate place it puts A's whole book in quotation marks in place of the parenthetical remark. No circularity here, or hint of a cheat. *Our* story of this counterfactual world might be complete, whether or not A's story is. But isn't the *content* of our book the same as the content of the book in A's library? (If so, we could save a lot of trees by using A's more efficient method of telling the story.)

Of course the story A tells, even if comprehensive, will be told in a particular language. If B's story is also comprehensive, it will be equivalent to A's story—identical in content—but it might still tell the story in a different way. We should resist the temptation to think that it detracts from the absoluteness of the content of a representation if the representation doesn't present a pure proposition, detached from any means of expression. The search for a representation, freed from any means of representation, will face a dilemma that parallels the one posed by Williams for the absolute conception of reality. Paraphrasing Williams: what a statement says (the proposition it expresses) must be independent of any linguistic item that expresses it. But here we face a dilemma: either the pure proposition is entirely empty, specified only as "whatever it is that these linguistic items (in Russian, English, etc.) express". In this case, it no longer does the work that was expected of it. On the other hand, we may have some determinate way of saying what the statement says, but then it is open to the reflection that our characterization of the proposition, once more, is only one linguistic representation of it, and again we have no independent point of leverage for raising it into a pure proposition.

I trust that no one will take this dilemma seriously, in this bald form, but there are real problems in the vicinity. It is a recurrent problem, in all of the attempts to view the philosophical terrain from the middle, that we "have no independent point of leverage". We want to theorize about the relation between representations and their content, but of course we can do so only by using other representations. We need a conceptual distinction between the content of a representation and the vehicle in which that content rides, but there may be more than one way to make the distinction, and controversies about how to make it can interact with substantive issues about the subject matter that is represented. It is sometimes frustrating to have to start in the middle, but that is where we are.

2

Epistemic Possibilities and the Knowledge Argument

> Mary, Mary, solitary, how does your garden grow? With grey, grey grass and black, black shrubs, and dead white flowers all in a row.
>
> David Lodge, *Thinks*

Everybody knows about Mary. She is a brilliant scientist who has been confined since birth to a black and white room. She knows, from reading the black and white books that line the shelves of her room, all there is to know about the physics of color, and the neurophysiology of color vision, but she has never had the opportunity to see colors. Even though she knows all the relevant physical and biological science, there is still something she does not know, something that she will learn only when she first emerges from her room, and sees colored things: she doesn't know what it is like to see colors.

This story, told by Frank Jackson, provided the context for an argument that he gave, *the knowledge argument*, which goes roughly like this: The story seems to imply that a person might know all the relevant physical facts while remaining ignorant of certain further facts—facts about the qualitative character of visual experience. So there must be facts to be known that are not physical facts. But if there are facts that go beyond the physical facts, then materialism—the thesis that all facts are physical facts—is false.

It is a deceptively simple argument that raises a number of different issues. The conclusion is that a certain metaphysical thesis is false, and most of the responses to the argument have been attempts to rebut this conclusion by reconciling the thought experiment, in one way or another, with materialism. I will review some of those responses, but my main concern will be with issues that are independent of materialism, but that the story and the arguments about it force us to confront. I want to consider what the story, and some variations on it, might show us about our epistemic relation to our experience and about the relation between our experience and our knowledge more generally. And since the argument turns on the claim that there is some new *information* that Mary acquires when she leaves her room, evaluating the argument will require getting clear about what kind of things items of information and contents of belief might be.

It has been suggested that the knowledge argument is a non-starter, since it "illegitimately draws a *metaphysical* conclusion—that physicalism is false—from an *epistemic* premise—that physically omniscient Mary would not know everything."[1] The suggestion is not that there is something wrong, in general, with deriving metaphysical conclusions from epistemological premises. There is no mystery about how epistemological premises can have metaphysical consequences, since knowledge implies truth. Prima facie, at least, it is reasonable to take *facts* to be the things that

---

[1] Alex Byrne makes this claim in Byrne (2002), citing Terence Horgan. He dismisses the knowledge argument with this remark, but goes on to use the Mary story to raise a different problem.

are known. On this assumption, one can validly reason from an epistemological premise that Mary knows all the facts of kind K, but does not know the fact that P to the metaphysical conclusion that the fact that P is not a fact of kind K. And this seems to be roughly the form of the knowledge argument. The suggestion seems to be that distinctions between items of knowledge (facts, if that is what it is that is known) can be decoupled from metaphysical distinctions between the possible situations in which those facts obtain. There are a number of strategies for resisting Jackson's argument, and avoiding the anti-materialist conclusion, but they all attempt, in one way or another, this kind of decoupling: all reject the idea that Mary lacks a kind of information that distinguishes between possible ways the world might be, in itself.

I will look at three strategies: First, what has been called the Fregean solution holds that we need a notion of information, or content, that is more fine grained than one grounded in a distinction between possibilities. Second, Lewis's *ability hypothesis* rejects the idea that it is *information*, in any sense, that Mary lacks. What she lacks is certain abilities. The third strategy is to grant that Mary lacks a kind of information, but to deny that she lacks information about the world as it is in itself. What she lacks is a kind of indexical, or self-locating information—information about her place in the world, rather than about what the world is like in itself. I will argue that none of these responses succeed in resolving the puzzle, though I will suggest that the last strategy is pointing in the right direction. My main aim in this chapter will be to motivate the claim that to get clear about Mary's predicament, and to understand its lesson, we need to confront the fact that she lacks a piece of information, and that information should be understood in terms of distinctions between real possibilities. And while I think the analogy between Mary's predicament and the predicament of the person who lacks certain self-locating information is a helpful one, I will suggest that we need to rethink the notion of indexical or self-locating attitudes to see how it helps.

1. THE FREGEAN STRATEGY

What I am calling "the Fregean strategy" for responding to the knowledge argument rejects the premise that there is a fact that physically omniscient Mary fails to know. What she learns only after emerging from her room is not a new fact, but an old fact known in a new way.[2] Mary knew all about colors under one kind of mode of presentation, but not under the mode that presents colors visually.

This kind of response stands in need of a theory of senses or modes of presentation, and of the objects of knowledge and the contents of belief that will vindicate the idea that there are distinctions between objects of knowledge and between contents of thought that are more fine-grained than distinctions between possibilities. It is not obvious that Frege's own notion of sense will do this job. For Frege, what is presented by a thought is a truth value, rather than a fact, and more generally what is presented by a mode of presentation is an extension. One traditional way of understanding the distinctions between senses that present the same referent (an interpretation that fits many of Frege's examples) is the descriptivist interpretation: different sense of names with the same referent correspond to different definite descriptions of the referent, and the clearest cases are descriptions that pick out the same referent only contingently. Different thoughts, on this way of understanding the notion of sense, would be the senses of sentences with different truth conditions (though perhaps with the same truth *value*). Frege does suggest, at least at one point, that logically equivalent sentences (or at least sentences that are

---

[2] In putting the point this way, I am assuming that *facts* are individuated so that if two thoughts are necessarily equivalent, then they state the same fact. On this assumption, the idea is that thoughts (objects of the attitudes) are individuated more finely than the facts that render them true or false. One might instead individuate facts more finely, as suggested above. I am not sure whether the difference is more than terminological here, but my worries about the Fregean strategy will apply to either way of expressing it.

logically equivalent but not themselves logically true) express identical thoughts.[3]

There may be other ways of developing the notion of sense, though I know of no clear account of the basis of a distinction between thoughts with the same truth conditions, or more generally, of senses that necessarily determine the same referent. One worry about any such notion is that it may blur the line between the content of a representation and the relation between the representation and its content, or between the content and the accidental features of a vehicle that carries that content.

Even if thoughts or propositions cannot be identified with their truth conditions—with the way they distinguish between possibilities—it should be uncontroversial that they *have* truth conditions that are essential to them, and so however Fregean thoughts are individuated, any thought will determine a unique coarse-grained proposition (where by a "coarse-grained proposition" I mean a proposition that is individuated by its truth conditions, or by the set of possible worlds in which it is true). Suppose we have distinct Fregean thoughts that are necessarily equivalent. The challenge is to say exactly how they are different, and what role the difference plays in the explanation of the difference between a representational state with the one thought as its content, and a representational state of the same kind, but with the other thought as its content. The explanation must preserve the idea that the thought is the *content* of the representation, where it is essential to the idea of content that it be detachable from the speaker or thinker, from the act of speaking or thinking, and from the form in which the content is represented in speech or thought. This feature of content was required for our response to Bernard Williams's dilemma for the absolute conception of reality, discussed at the end of Chapter 1. It was acknowledged there that any representation represents the world from a particular perspective in the world, and has the

---

[3] See the letter from Frege to Husserl in Beaney (1997), 302.

content that it has only in virtue of its relation to the things in the world that are being represented. The claim was that this is not a problem for a conception of the world as it is in itself so long as we can separate, conceptually, the content of the representation from the parochial features of the situation that account for its having the content that it has.

But whatever Fregean thoughts are, it is not clear in any case that appeal to them can avoid the conclusion that the kind of ignorance that Mary has involves an inability to rule out certain possibilities. For suppose there are two Fregean thoughts that even a logically omniscient thinker might grasp without realizing that they have the same truth-value. Suppose, that is, that no amount of a priori reasoning could lead a thinker from one to the other. In such a case, it seems that one might form a clear and coherent conception of a situation in which one of the thoughts is true, and the other false, and this seems to imply that such a situation would be a *conceptual* possibility.

Now let me try to connect this with Mary's situation. (I will talk, in this discussion, about *concepts*, intending by this term something like a Fregean sense of a predicative expression, the mode of presentation of a property. I will later express doubts about whether we know what we are talking about when we talk about concepts, and so doubts about whether we should put any theoretical weight on such a notion, but I assume that the Fregean will understand what I am supposing, even if I do not.) With her vast scientific knowledge, Mary will have a concept of the type of functional–physiological state that she would be in when having an experience of seeing something red—call that concept ψ. Call the phenomenal concept[4] that she acquires only when

---

[4] There is a vast literature about phenomenal concepts, how they relate to descriptive concepts, demonstrative concepts, and the phenomenal experiences themselves. See, for example, Sturgeon (1994), Loar (1990), Tye (2003), Stoljar (2005), and the papers in Alter and Walter (2007). I will have a little more to say about them in Chapter 5.

she leaves her room and sees red, ϕ. Now distinguish these two Fregean thoughts: (a) the one expressed by "Mary is having a ψ experience", and (b) the one expressed by "Mary is having a ϕ experience". It would seem that these are two thoughts that meet our condition: no amount of a priori reasoning would suffice to infer either from the other. Of course Mary, when still in her room, is not in a position to grasp the concept ϕ, and so not in a position to entertain thought (b), but that does not matter to the point.[5] The fact remains that a person who *was* in a position to grasp both concept ϕ and concept ψ would still not be able to reason from (a) to (b), or vice versa. Mary might come to know (b), after leaving her room, and still not be in a position to know whether (a) is true. And even after leaving her room, and acquiring the concept ϕ, she still could not make the hypothetical inference from (a) to (b). (We could grant that if (a) is in fact true—if Mary is in fact having a ψ experience—then she will know that (b) is true—that she is having a ϕ experience. But she will not know it by inference from (a).) So however Fregean modes of presentation are individuated, it seems that the story about Mary supports the conclusion that there are at least *conceptually* possible situations that differ even when those situations are physically indiscernible.

For the knowledge argument to go through, we would need a further controversial inference, one that has received a great deal of discussion in the literature:[6] an inference from conceptual possibility to metaphysical possibility. But if there is a distinction to be made here, it needs explanation, and there are several very different ways of explaining it. In the background are different

---

[5] Daniel Stoljar (1995) makes the point that it does not suffice to dissolve the puzzle about Mary to note that Mary lacks the relevant phenomenal concept. To argue this, he uses a variation on the story of Mary in which Mary has had the experience, and has the phenomenal concept, but still lacks the ability to make the inference from the physical description of her state to the phenomenal description.

[6] For some of this literature, and further references, see the papers in Hawthorne and Szabo Gendler (2002). I discuss the issue in Stalnaker (2004a).

general views about the relation between possibilities and the conceptual resources that we use to characterize and discriminate between them.

Some may be inclined to start with some kind of representational vehicles (such as *concepts*, on one way of construing this notion) and to understand possible worlds as complex constructions built out of these resources. Conceptually possible worlds are characterizations of a world that are conceptually coherent: those that a thinker who is competent with the constitutive concepts would judge to be possible. The metaphysically possible worlds are those that meet some further substantive conditions: constraints, not on the coherence of the *concepts*, but on the compatibility of the *properties* that the concepts pick out, or on the potentialities of the things to which the concepts refer. On an alternative picture, which I think gives a clearer account of the phenomena, we begin with a space of possibilities, and explain the content of a thinker's representational resources in terms of the ways in which those resources are used to discriminate between the possibilities. The possibilities we begin with are characterized in terms of the things and kinds of things that would exist and the properties and relations that would be exemplified if those possibilities were realized, and are not constituted by anything conceptual or representational. The theorists who begin in this way with the possibilities, referring to them in order to talk about the conceptual capacities of the thinkers they are theorizing about, will of course be using their own conceptual resources to characterize them, but we cannot conclude from this that what they are talking about is thereby itself conceptual, any more than we could conclude that rocks are conceptual from the fact that the geologist uses conceptual resources to theorize about them. Metaphysical possibility, on this second picture, is possibility in the widest sense. If the theorist judges that her subject really can conceive of a situation in which a certain proposition is true, then she should conclude that there must be a (metaphysically possible) situation in which that proposition is true.

Let's look more closely at the kind of situation that is alleged to be conceptually, but not metaphysically possible. A situation in which the concept ϕ applies to something to which the concept ψ fails to apply is deemed metaphysically impossible (by the materialist) because according to the materialist's thesis, the two concepts determine the same *property*, so there cannot be a metaphysical possibility in which one of the concepts applies while the other does not. But one might respond that even though the concepts *in fact* determine the same property, it is not (metaphysically) impossible that they should determine different properties. If we really succeed in conceiving of a situation in which one concept applies while the other does not, then we are conceiving of a situation in which the property picked out by the one is different from the property picked out by the other. The Fregean might insist that it is essential to a concept that it pick out the property it in fact picks out, so that a conceptually possible situation in which, for example, the concept "aluminum" picks out a substance that is not an element, is not a metaphysically possible situation, but note that we are now talking about the metaphysics of concepts, and not the metaphysics of the kinds and properties that the concepts pick out.

I am not sure what concepts are, or exactly how the cognitive abilities that constitute the possession of concepts should be spelled out, but it seems to me puzzling if the following is possible: one might be fully competent with each of two concepts, and be able to form a clear and coherent conception of a situation in which one is exemplified, and the other is not, even though there is no possible situation in which one is exemplified and the other is not. I would expect conceptual capacities to be explained in terms of the ability to form accurate conceptions of possible situations in which they are exemplified. There are, of course, the notorious cases of necessary a posteriori truths (such as that aluminum is an element), which are cases in which it appears that one can form a coherent conception of a situation in which the statement is false, even though there is no possible world in which it is false. The philosopher who rejects the idea that metaphysical possibility is a restriction on a wider notion of conceptual possibility recognizes the need to account for this kind of "illusion of possibility".[7] His general strategy is to explain them as cases in which one is conceiving of a genuine metaphysical possibility, but misdescribing it as a case in which the statement in question is false. The possibility is one in which a different substance plays the role that aluminum plays in the actual world. But it is not clear that the apparent divergence between Mary's theoretical concept and her later acquired phenomenal concept can be explained in this way. So the Fregean strategy does not promise to defuse our puzzle, at least not without a lot of further development.

(The evaluation of the Fregean strategy takes us back to some old issues, first raised in Kripke's arguments against the identity theory in *Naming and Necessity*. We will come back to some of them in a different form.)

2. THE ABILITY HYPOTHESIS

David Lewis argued that we can avoid the anti-materialist conclusion of the knowledge argument, and the hypothesis of phenomenal information, only by adopting a more radical solution, since he granted that distinctions of informational content require distinctions between metaphysical possibilities. The radical solution, which he called "the ability hypothesis", holds that what Mary acquires, on leaving her room, is not any kind of information at all, but only certain abilities, for example the ability to recognize colors, and to imagine seeing them.[8]

---

[7] See Stalnaker (2003a), Jackson (1998), and Yablo (2006) for discussion of this issue.

[8] Lewis (1988). See also Nemirow (1990).

Is the ability hypothesis plausible? Lewis would agree that knowledge of any kind is a kind of capacity or ability; it is just that certain abilities—*cognitive* abilities—are aptly described in terms of the possession of *information*, where information is explained in terms of alternative possibilities. The plausibility of the ability hypothesis hangs on whether the abilities in question that Mary lacks before leaving her room are of this kind. Can Mary's ignorance be represented as the failure to exclude certain possibilities? In defending the hypothesis, Lewis argued that there were none to be found:

When someone doesn't know what it's like to have an experience, where are the alternative open possibilities? I cannot present to myself in thought a range of alternative possibilities about what it might be like to taste Vegemite. That is because I cannot imagine either what it *is* like to taste Vegemite, or any alternative way that it *might* be like but in fact isn't. . . . I can't even pose the question that phenomenal information is supposed to answer: is it this way or that? It seems that the alternative possibilities must be unthinkable beforehand; and afterwards too, except for the one that turns out to be actualized.[9]

It is a relevant fact that the subject cannot present the alternative possibilities to himself in thought, but this is not a reason to think that the possibilities are not there. The role of alternative possibilities in the characterization of information is an external one: the theorist distinguishes possibilities, and uses them to describe another's state of mind. Possible situations that cannot be distinguished by the subject may still be relevant for characterizing that subject's cognitive capacities and limitations. For example: Mary, remarkably, has never heard of Margaret Thatcher. (All that intensive study of color science left her little time for learning about political history.) So she doesn't know that Margaret Thatcher was Prime Minister of Great Britain for many years. *We* can see that possible worlds in which Thatcher was Prime

---

[9] Lewis (1988), 281.

Minister, possible worlds in which she was not, and possible worlds in which she was never born are all among Mary's epistemic possibilities, but she cannot represent these possibilities to herself, cannot distinguish them from each other. Is Mary's ignorance of what it is like to see colors (or Lewis's ignorance of the taste of Vegemite) like this?

After the fact (after she learns about Margaret Thatcher) Mary can represent to herself the possibilities that she previously could not distinguish between ("for all I knew before, Margaret Thatcher might never have existed"). The situation is similar with her retrospective characterization, after leaving the room, of her prior ignorance of color experience ("For all I knew before I left the room, red might have looked like *this* [demonstrating in imagination the way green looks to her] rather than like *that* [demonstrating in imagination the way red looks to her]"). It does seem that the abilities Mary lacks are *cognitive* abilities that one should expect to be representable in terms of information of some kind. While it may be right, as the ability hypothesis claims, that Mary does not necessarily acquire information merely by having color experience, it seems that she does acquire an ability to make distinctions between possibilities that she could not distinguish before, and a proper account of these abilities requires an account of the distinctions between the possibilities. So I don't think that the ability hypothesis, by itself, will give us a way of avoiding a distinctive kind of phenomenal information.

3. THE SELF-LOCATION ANALOGY

Recall our simple version of the form of the knowledge argument: one can know all of the facts of kind K without knowing the fact that P; therefore, the fact that P is not a fact of kind K. The self-location analogy begins by noting that the phenomenon of essentially indexical or self-locating thought seems to support a premise of the same form: one may know all of the relevant objective facts about the world as it is in itself, without knowing certain facts about who one is, or what time it is. But the parallel conclusion (that, for example, the facts expressed by Lingens at noon that he is Lingens, and that it was then noon are not objective facts) does not seem to support a metaphysical thesis that parallels the conclusion drawn in the knowledge argument. Few are tempted to try to explain this distinctive kind of knowledge by refining our metaphysical conception of the objective world—by objectifying the self.[10] One might try to see how the metaphysical inference is blocked in this case, and whether this might offer insight into how it might be blocked in the case of the argument about knowledge of phenomenal experience. I think the analogy is a useful one that does help to sharpen the issue about phenomenal information, but it remains controversial exactly how self-locating knowledge and information should be understood, and we will need to get clearer about that before exploring the parallels. I will look briefly at the way that John Perry uses the analogy, and then consider in the next chapter how I think we should understand our knowledge of and beliefs about who and where we are.

Just as the case for irreducible phenomenal knowledge is based on a thought experiment (the story of Mary), so the case for irreducible self-locating knowledge is based on examples, some fanciful and some more mundane. There are stories told by Hector-Neri Castaneda, John Perry, David Kaplan, David Lewis, among others to illustrate the fact that our knowledge of ourselves and our place in the world—knowledge about what is happening

---

[10] Not everyone avoids this temptation. Kit Fine discusses a thesis that he calls "First-personal realism" that holds that "reality is not exhausted by the 'objective' or impersonal facts," and Caspar Hare considers a view that he calls "egocentric presentism". See Fine (2005) and Hare (2007). Thomas Nagel develops a notion he calls "the objective self", but he does not intend this to be a feature of an impersonal metaphysical conception of the world, and in fact argues that refining our impersonal conception would not help to explain the distinctive kind of information. See Nagel (1986).

now, or *here*, or to *me*—cannot be reduced to impersonal objective knowledge about what the world, as it is in itself, is like. There is John Perry's supermarket shopper who follows a trail of spilled sugar to find the person spilling it before discovering that it is himself.[11] There is the case of the person who knows, at noon, that the meeting starts at noon, but does not get up to go to it, since she does not know that the meeting starts *now*. There are various stories about amnesiacs who know all about themselves without realizing that it is themselves that they know about, and then there is David Lewis's story of two omniscient gods, each of whom allegedly knows exactly what possible world he is in, but not which of the two gods he himself is.[12] But how should we understand the distinctive kind of information that these stories illustrate?

Perry calls it *"reflexive content"*, and distinguishes it from what he calls *"subject matter content"*. (The label may be misleading; as we will see, it is unclear from Perry's examples whether the distinction is really between two kinds of content, or just between two kinds of things that a thought might be about.) Reflexive content is information about the relation between a representation and its ordinary subject matter content. He illustrates the distinction between subject matter and reflexive content with the following example: Perry is at a party, talking to Fred Dretske, whose work he knows well, but who he has never met before. In the course of the conversation, Perry recommends that his interlocutor, who he does not realize is Dretske, read a book he admires, *Knowledge and the Flow of Information*. Although Perry already knew that Dretske wrote this book, he learns something new when Dretske says to him, "I wrote *Knowledge and the Flow of Information*." What he already knew was the *subject matter content* of what he was told—the singular proposition about Dretske that he wrote that book. The new information that he acquired, information that

[11] Perry (1979).   [12] Lewis (1979).

was conveyed by the statement, is information about the relation between the representation (the statement) and its (subject matter) content. This is the *reflexive content* of the statement.

This distinction, according to Perry's diagnosis, is the key to dissolving Jackson's puzzle. The knowledge argument relies on what he calls "the subject matter assumption," an assumption that involves a conflation of the two kinds of content. To make the subject matter assumption is to commit the *subject matter fallacy*. Once we reject this assumption, he argues, we will have no more trouble from Mary. Just as in the Dretske example, Perry already knew the subject matter content of what he was told, so in the case of Mary, she already knew, when still in her room, the subject matter content of the statement with which she might express the new belief that she acquires: "seeing red is like *this*", where the "this" refers to a type of experience. What she did not already know was a different piece of information, which is the reflexive content of that statement.

The subject matter assumption, as Perry states it, is this:

The rational content of a belief is that part of the full truth conditions of the belief that accounts for the role the belief has in theoretical and practical inferences. The rational content of a belief is the conditions its truth puts on the subject matter of the belief, the objects the notions and concepts in the belief are of.[13]

The subject matter *fallacy* is "the fallacy of supposing that *the* content of a statement or a belief consists in the conditions that the truth of the statement or belief puts on the objects and properties the statement or belief is about."[14]

These characterizations presuppose that statements and beliefs are things of the same kind, which I think is a mistake. What kind of object are we talking about when we talk about someone's belief? There are several things one might mean: first, one might be referring to the content believed: Bert's belief about who is

[13] Perry (1999), 113–14.   [14] Ibid., 20.

President, if he believes that George W. Bush is the President, is the proposition that George W. Bush is the President. If Alice also believes this, then her belief about the matter is the same as his, in the literal sense that the two beliefs are identical. Alternatively, one might mean, by Bert's belief that George W. Bush is the President, the fact that Bert believes this, or perhaps the state of having this belief (a state that both Bert and Alice are in). In these senses, too, the belief is individuated by its content, and not by some vehicle that expresses the content. In either of these senses, it would make no sense to talk about two different kinds of content of *a belief*, even if the distinction is clear for utterances or statements.

As I understand Perry's distinction, reflexive content is a relative notion: the reflexive content of one utterance might be the subject matter content of a different utterance. For example, the reflexive content of Dretske's utterance, "I wrote *Knowledge and the Flow of Information*", is the subject-matter content expressed by a different utterance, such as one that John Perry might have produced on the occasion: "The person talking to me wrote *Knowledge and the Flow of Information*." The first statement, unlike the second, makes no claim about anyone saying anything. In one sense, its truth condition requires only that Dretske have written that book. But in another sense, it is a condition on the truth of the utterance that it be produced by the author of that book, and this condition will be satisfied only if the statement is made. The distinction, applied to utterances, is reasonably clear, but to apply it to states of knowledge or belief we need to assume a linguistic model of such mental states, and to apply the distinction either to the mental sentences that are presumed to reside in the belief box, or perhaps to the sentences that the knower or believer would most naturally use to express his knowledge or belief. But even if one were to take the notorious belief box myth seriously, who knows in what particular form Mary might store the information she receives, and how can that be relevant? The puzzle about Mary is a puzzle about the nature of the information itself, and not about the way it is represented or expressed.

Perry sketches a metaphorical model of an internal mechanism that might underlie the cognitive events that take place in the Dretske example, as well as in the case of Mary—a model that is a little different from the belief box picture, but similar in spirit. In the Dretske case, there is a perceptual buffer containing a notion of a person currently being perceived, and a file of information associated with a standing notion of Fred Dretske. What happens when Perry learns who he is talking to is that a plug from the former is connected to a socket from the latter, allowing information to flow between them. The model for the cognitive event that takes place when Mary leaves her room is similar: she has a quasi-perceptual buffer which, when she is looking at something red, gives her "access" to an internal state about which she has a standing notion, associated with a rich file of information. When she connects them, she knows what it is like to see red.

(A parenthetical remark: I am suspicious of these models of representational mechanisms, with their boxes, buffers and files, since they tend to mix intentional and non-intentional description in a way that may give an illusion of explanation of intentionality where there is none. There are these file folders that contain, not pieces of paper, but *information*. But in fact, when one opens a folder, one doesn't find *a proposition* between the covers; one needs an explanation of what it is that gives whatever is literally in there the intentional content that it has, and the metaphor may help to obscure the fact that one is needed.)

But in any case, even if something like this is what happens, the information that Perry receives when he learns who he is talking with, and that Mary receives when she learns what it is like to see red, is not information about the cognitive mechanism. They can only speculate about that. In the Dretske case, what Perry learns is a fact about the world: that the person he is talking to is Fred Dretske. This is an unproblematic piece of contingent information that can be characterized independently of any mechanism by which it is represented. When Perry received this information, he updated his beliefs by excluding certain possibilities that were compatible with his prior beliefs—those in which the person he was talking to was someone other than Dretske.

The case is similar in this respect to some other examples of reflexive content that Perry gives. Consider, for example, his case of the Russian pasta chef with an imperfect grasp of English who is taking a class on cooking pasta. He knows perfectly well how long to cook each kind of pasta, but not what they are called in English. When he is told "cook vermicelli for four minutes, and linguini for six", he already knew the subject matter content of the claim, but learns some facts about English terminology, which are part of the reflexive content of the statement: that "vermicelli" and "linguini", respectively, refer to vermicelli and linguini. No need to talk about buffers, files, or internal representation, or even about the particular utterance in question. One can describe the information that the Russian pasta cook acquires by describing the possible worlds that were compatible with his prior state of knowledge that he subsequently excluded: they are possible worlds in which the semantics of English is slightly different, with the words "linguini" and "vermicelli" interchanged.

Perry suggests at one point that thinking of content in terms of possible worlds tends to promote the subject matter fallacy: "Possible-worlds semantics and concepts like 'rigid designation' are oriented toward the subject matter truth-conditions of statements; to suppose that they can be used, without supplementation, to characterize belief and knowledge . . . is to commit the subject matter fallacy."[15] But in fact, the possible worlds framework is ideally suited to represent the distinctive kind of reflexive information that Perry is talking about, and has been used to represent it.

[15] Perry (1999), 172–3. Perry does go on to say that "this does not mean that possible worlds themselves are useless in characterizing belief and knowledge".

Possible worlds represent totalities of facts, including facts about speakers and thinkers, and the circumstances that give their speech and thought its content. The framework provides the resources to represent any kind of information in terms of distinctions between the possibilities, and we can say what a proposition is "about" (what its real subject matter is) by saying how the worlds in which it is true differ from the worlds in which it is false. The framework provides the resources to abstract the content from the vehicle, even in the case of reflexive information, since we can describe the relevant distinctions between the possibilities from the theorist's external point of view.

Most of Perry's examples of reflexive information fit the pattern that I have used the possible worlds framework, and what I called "the diagonalization strategy", to try to clarify.[16] One is a case of a boyhood friend of Bill Clinton (call him Joe) who knew Clinton as Bill Blythe, and does not realize that his old friend is the President, Bill Clinton. He knows that Bill Blythe was born in Arkansas, but does not realize that Bill Clinton was. "How can this be so?" The diagonalization strategy begins by asking what (according to the story) the world is like, according to Joe. We try to describe, in our own terms, a world that fits Joe's conception of the way the world might be, for all he knows. The answer to this question is pretty clear, up to a point: there is a world compatible with Joe's knowledge in which the person who is the current President, and who is named "Bill Clinton" is a different person from the one that Joe knew as a child. In this world, the second of these people was born in Arkansas, but the first was not. (Which of the two is the real Bill Clinton, and so also the real Bill Blythe? The answer to this question is not so clear, but it may not matter). Second, we ask, how is it that the sentence "Bill Clinton was born in Arkansas" can be used to communicate

---

[16] See the papers in Stalnaker (1999) and Stalnaker (2004) for my development and application of this strategy.

new information to Joe by excluding this possibility, while "Bill Blythe was born in Arkansas" would not do so? The answer to this second question begins by noting that even if those two sentences, on their standard interpretation, *in fact* express the same singular proposition, the same sentences, *as used in the world in question*, will express different propositions, assuming that they are interpreted in the standard way, as singular propositions about the person named. The proposition expressed by the former is false in the situation, while the proposition expressed by the latter is true. The diagonal proposition is the function from possible worlds to truth values that takes as its truth value relative to world x the truth value that the sentence in question would have, if expressed in world x. I think this story gives a perspicuous representation of this example and others, and that it fits with much of what Perry says about them.

Perry acknowledges that situations such as Joe's can be usefully modeled using possible worlds, but insists that the "possible worlds in question . . . need to deal with names, concepts, notions, utterances, and other paraphernalia of thought and language, and not simply with the subject matter the thought and language are about."[17] We can agree that the relation between the subject and what he is thinking about will play a role in the characterization of his cognitive situation, but we need to make no claims or commitments about his mechanisms of mental representation. The differences between the actual world and the world as Joe takes it to be are mainly differences in what is going on in his environment, not in what is going on in his head. In most cases where the diagonalization strategy applies (and most cases that Perry would describe as cases involving reflexive content), the differences between the relevant contrasting possible worlds will be partly semantic and partly extra-semantic, and so the real subject matter of the information will be a corresponding mix. The

[17] Perry (1999), 173.

possible worlds representation of information, and the diagonalization strategy makes it easy to represent the way the two kinds of information interact.

So I agree with Perry that a notion of reflexive information, properly understood, is a useful one, and I will agree that it is relevant to clarifying Mary's situation, but I don't think that simply recognizing the distinction between subject matter and reflexive content will dissolve the puzzle. There are several problems with the analogy between cases like Dretske's and Joe's and the case of Mary.

To see the first problem, it is useful to divide Mary's cognitive achievement, when she learns what it is like to see red, into two stages: first, she has the experience of seeing red, and then she learns that it is red that she is seeing (connecting her experience with all of the information about the color, and about the internal physiological states involved in experiencing it). Perry himself makes this division, in effect, using the device of what he calls the "Nida-Rümelin room" after a variation on the story of Mary told by Martine Nida-Rümelin.[18] This is a room wallpapered with random shapes of various colors, but with no recognizable colored objects. In Nida-Rümelin's variation, Mary (or Nida-Rümelin's alternative character, who is named Marianne) learns what it is like to see red, and the other colors, by moving to this room, but she remains ignorant of which colors she is seeing. It is at stage one that the problematic cognitive achievement—the learning "what it is like" to see red—takes place. But it is at stage two that plugs are connected to sockets; it is only at this point that Mary receives information that *this* color is red, the information that is analogous to the information that Perry received, that *this* person is Dretske. So even if the analogy could help to explain what is learned at stage two, it is not clear that this would be relevant to the original puzzle.

[18] See Nida-Rümelin (1995). The aim of her variation is to distinguish these "two steps of [Mary's] epistemic progress." Cf. Daniel Stoljar's discussion of "Experienced Mary" in Stoljar (1995).

But even at stage two, there seems to be a disanalogy. In the Dretske case, the fact that was learned was a straightforward contingent fact. The possibilities excluded were possibilities in which Perry was talking to some person other than Dretske. When Mary learns, at stage two, that *this* experience is an experience of red, is what she learns a contingent fact? It was compatible with Perry's prior knowledge that he was talking to someone other than Dretske, but is it compatible with Mary's prior knowledge (her knowledge at stage one, after having seen red things, but before learning that they are red) that she is having an experience of a different kind? There is at least a prima facie reason to think that the analogy breaks down at this point. Perry's prior perceptual notion or concept of Dretske—the notion or concept that is the intentional content of what is in the perceptual buffer—is clearly a nonrigid notion: a notion that may apply to different individuals in different possible worlds. That is just to say that in certain nonactual possible worlds (some of which are compatible with Perry's prior beliefs) the person he is seeing and talking with is someone else. But is it plausible to assume that the *phenomenal* notion or concept that Mary acquired at stage one is nonrigid in the same way: that the same notion may apply to different experiences in different possible worlds? I will later be arguing that this is indeed compatible with Mary's stage one knowledge, but I will also be arguing that biting this bullet requires that we question some entrenched dogmas about the relation between phenomenal experience and knowledge. At this point, I just want to note this prima facie problem with the analogy.

So I don't agree with Perry that we can dissolve the puzzle raised by the knowledge argument simply by making a distinction between subject matter and reflexive content, and by bringing to the surface and rejecting the assumption that all content is subject matter content. But I do agree that the recognition of information that essentially involves the representor and his or her place in the world is required to clarify the problem. Both phenomenal knowledge and self-locating knowledge are, in some sense, essentially subjective, and both raise questions about the relation between an objective conception of the world and a subject's perspective on it. I will come back to the story of Mary in Chapter 4, but first I want to try to make clear exactly how we should understand self-locating attitudes, a problem that is of interest in itself, and that will be relevant to some of the issues about knowledge of content that I want to talk about later, as well as to Jackson's vexing puzzle. So in the next chapter I will sketch the way I think self-locating knowledge and belief should be represented.

3

Locating Ourselves in the World

Consider the case of the two gods. They inhabit a certain possible world, and they know exactly what world it is. Therefore they know every proposition that is true at their world. Insofar as knowledge is a propositional attitude, they are omniscient. Still I can imagine them to suffer ignorance: neither one knows which of the two he is.

David Lewis[1]

John Perry argued that we need to recognize a kind of representational content—reflexive content—that essentially involves the subject who is doing the representing, and her relation to what is being represented. And he argued that distinguishing this kind of content from *subject matter content* will dissolve the puzzle about Mary. I agree with Perry that it will help, at least to clarify the puzzle, to be explicit about the role of the subject's perspective in the representation of content, but it remains unclear exactly what reflexive content is. My aim in this chapter is to sketch an account of self-locating belief that I hope will begin to make sense of a notion of informational content that is not detachable from

[1] Lewis (1979), 139.

the situation of a subject, or from a context in which the content is ascribed. Perry's discussion made use of a model of a representational mechanism—a form that internal representations might take. The account I will sketch focuses on the informational content of the representation, trying to be as neutral as possible about the means by which content is stored or expressed. With both ordinary beliefs about the objective world, and self-locating beliefs, we will be concerned with truth conditions: with what conditions a world must meet in order for a believer to have a correct conception of the world. And in keeping with the general anti-Cartesian strategy, the content of a subject's beliefs will be characterized from an external perspective. Theorists, or attributors, use their own resources to describes the world as the subject takes it to be. That is, they describe the world according to the subject in terms of the things, events, properties and relations that they find in the actual world.

1. CENTERED WORLDS PROPOSITIONS

We start, on this approach, with the classical possible-worlds representation of a state of belief or knowledge as a set of possible worlds, the doxastically or epistemically accessible worlds, those that are compatible with the subject's beliefs or knowledge. This kind of representation is highly idealized, but the idealization does not avoid or evade the particular problems we want to focus on, and will help to sharpen the issues. The problem is how to generalize or modify the classical model to take account of essentially indexical or self-locating belief and knowledge.

If our question is, exactly when are self-locating statements and beliefs true, then the answer is clear and unproblematic: A statement of the form "I am F" is true, when said or thought by x, if and only if x is F. So if David Kaplan says "my pants are on fire", what he says is true if and only if David Kaplan's pants are on fire at the time at which he says it. But this answer does not tell us what the *contents* of the statements are—what *information* they convey, what belief they express, what kind of *fact*, if any, they state. The reason we cannot straightforwardly infer from this account of the truth conditions of the statement or belief to the content is that the facts that determine the truth value may play two different roles: to determine *what* is said, and to determine *whether* what is said is true or false. These truth conditions give us the content of the statement only if it is assumed that the statement has the same content on each occasion of use.

One influential answer to the question of content, defended by David Lewis, is this: If the contents of ordinary beliefs about objective facts can be represented by sets of possible worlds, then the contents of self-locating beliefs can be represented by sets of *centered* possible worlds, where a centered possible world is a pair consisting of a world plus a center, which is a designated time and person. Since "I am sad" is true if and only if it is said or thought by a sad person, its content will be represented by the set of centered possible worlds that have a sad person at their designated center. The content of "the meeting is about to start" will be the set of centered worlds at which the meeting in question takes place soon after the time that is designated as the center.[2]

This elegant modification of the standard account is a generalization, since as Lewis observed, ordinary beliefs about the objective world can be represented as a special case of self-locating beliefs, beliefs where the centers are irrelevant. Beliefs that might be expressed with eternal sentences, such as my belief that pigs can't fly, have as their content the set of centered worlds,

---

[2] Lewis's theory is spelled out in detail in Lewis (1979). In his formulation of the theory, it is *properties* that are the contents of belief, where properties are identified with sets of possible individuals. To account for the temporal dimension, it is assumed that it is not continuant individuals, but time-slices of individuals to which beliefs are ascribed. Given the assumptions of Lewis's general framework, there will be a one–one correspondence between properties in his sense and sets of centered possible worlds.

<c,w> such that it is false that pigs can fly in w.

Lewis's account modifies the standard possible worlds account by replacing possible worlds, throughout, with centered worlds. A belief state is a set of centered worlds, and the contents ascribed when one ascribes a belief are represented by sets of centered worlds.

There are a number of problems with this account of self-locating content. First, this account identifies contents that ought to be distinguished. What I believe when I believe that I was born in New Jersey is something about myself, something different from what my fellow New Jersey natives believe about themselves. What I tell the waiter when I tell him that I will have the mushroom soufflé is different from what you tell the waiter if you decide to have the same thing. But on the centered worlds account, our respective beliefs and statements have the same content. Now there are different ways of classifying states of belief, and there is nothing wrong with categorizing belief states so that self-ascriptions of the same property count as the same, in one sense. (If Alice believes that she will win the election, and Bert believes that he will win, then in a sense, they both believe the same thing.) But if one thinks of this as classifying by *content*, the result is that the contents of belief are not true or false in themselves, but only true or false relative to a speaker or thinker and a time. It is natural to allow that sentence or utterance types might be true or false only relative to a situation in which they are used, but this is natural because it is natural to say that the content expressed by a sentence or utterance type may be different from context to context. It seems less natural to say that the content of a belief might be true for one believer and false for another. Second, and more important, Lewis's account distinguishes contents that ought to be identified. If Rudolf Lingens tell you that he is sad, or that he is Rudolf Lingens, and you understand and accept what he says, then it seems that the information you acquire is the same information that he imparted. But you do not, of course, thereby ascribe the property of being sad, or of being Rudolf Lingens to yourself. This problem with the account is more significant, since we need to be able to compare and contrast the beliefs and other attitudes of different subjects—to represent agreement and disagreement—in order to understand communication. The Lewis centered-worlds account provides no distinction between a difference in perspective and a disagreement. And the fact that the contents of belief are tied to a time (the time of the center) also makes it more difficult to understand the way the beliefs of a single believer change over time. The account provides no distinction between a change in belief that is a change of mind and a change that results from a change in the facts. (I may stop believing that it is raining because it stops raining, or because I learn that I was mistaken. In the former case, it may be that I still believe what I believed before—that it was raining at the time—and one wants an account of the content of tensed beliefs that allows for this.)

A misleading picture sometimes accompanies the Lewis account of self-locating belief: belief about what possible world you are in is like belief about what country you are in, while beliefs about where in the world you are is like a more specific belief about where, in the country you are (what village, street corner, or mountain top). But ordinary belief about where you are in the world is always also belief about what possible world you are in (what possible state of the world is actual). If I am not sure, as I drive along the highway toward New York, whether I am still in Massachusetts, then I am not sure whether I am in a possible world in which *this* stretch of highway is located in Massachusetts. If I know that the meeting starts at noon, but not whether it starts *now*, then I don't know whether or not I am in a world where I am sitting in my office thinking this thought at noon, or in a world where I am thinking it at some earlier time. The misleading picture is encouraged by the imagery of Lewis's modal realism (according to which possible worlds are literally places where people are located), but also by the character of some of the examples used to make the point that beliefs can be irreducibly indexical. Often, to nail the point down, the example will be a case where there are two scenarios within a single possible world involving different people, places or times (two amnesiacs lost in different libraries, or the two omniscient gods). The people in the scenarios know (in each situation) all of the relevant *objective* facts about them, but remain ignorant of which of the actual situations they are in fact in. That is, they know what world they are in, but not where in it they are. But a story of this kind needs to be highly contrived if it is to work: the internal mental perspectives of the two subjects, or of the subject at the two times, need to be indiscernible from each other. But it is important to note that this science fiction element is entirely unnecessary to make the point that self-locating information is irreducible to information about the objective world. Even if no one else in the actual world is, was or will be experiencing the thoughts and feelings that you are now experiencing, and even if the objective description of the world includes a description of which people are having which thoughts and feelings at which times, you still cannot infer from the objective description where you are in the world, and what time it is now. You need to put the objective information together with your knowledge that it is *you* who are experiencing these thoughts and feelings, and that it is *now* that you are experiencing them.[3]

2. A MODIFIED CENTERED WORLDS ACCOUNT

In the modification of Lewis's account that I will propose, it will be assumed that ignorance of where one is in the world is *always* also ignorance of what world is actual. Even if an experience just

[3] Lewis makes this point. See Lewis (1979), 138–9.

like *this* one is taking place at two times in the actual world, and I don't know which of the two times is *now*, the world in which *this* token experience is taking place at a different time is a different (uncentered) world.

To set up the modified account that I think will give a more adequate representation of self-locating content, let me start by distinguishing two questions:

(1) How should a person's state of belief as a whole be represented so that it includes his or her self-locating beliefs?
(2) What is the content of a self-locating belief?

In the classical formal semantic models for knowledge and belief that ignores the phenomenon of self-location, a belief state as a whole is represented by a set of possible worlds (the epistemic or doxastic alternatives), and the content of a particular belief is also represented by a set of worlds: x believes that ϕ if and only if the set of worlds representing x's belief state is included in the set of worlds in which the proposition that ϕ is true. The Lewis account tells a parallel story, with centered worlds replacing worlds, leaving the structure of the theory exactly the same. In both cases, the representation of a belief state, and the contents ascribed, are abstracted from the believer. But in my view, the lesson we should learn from the phenomenon of self-locating belief is that we cannot give an adequate representation of a state of belief without connecting the world as the subject takes it to be with the subject who has the beliefs. What we want to represent is the state of belief that a particular individual x is in at a particular time t in a particular possible world w. When we represent the way this individual locates himself in the world as he takes it to be, we need to include the information about who it is who is locating himself there, and we need to link the world as the believer takes it to be to the world in which the believer takes the world to be that way.

To model a knowledge or belief state, I will use the same resources that Lewis uses—centered possible worlds—but the role of the centering will be slightly different than it is in Lewis's theory. A belief state will be represented by a pair consisting of a centered world (representing the believer and time and world in which the believer is in the belief state) and a set of centered worlds (representing the ways the world might be, according to that believer, the time that, for all he believes, it might be, and the person that, for all he believes, he might be). Call the world that is the first term of this pair "the *base* (centered) *world* ". The centered worlds in the set that is the second term are the *belief worlds*. The role of the centers is to link the believer, and time of belief, to the possible worlds that are the way that the believer takes the world to be at that time, and to represent where, in those worlds, he takes himself to be.

The information about the belief states of a range of believers at various times in different worlds can be encoded by a doxastic accessibility relation, as in a standard Kripke model for a logic of knowledge or belief (of the kind first developed by Jaakko Hintikka). But in a Hintikka-style model, there is an accessibility relation for each subject, and presumably for each time, whereas in the model I am proposing, the subject and time are built into the relata, rather than the relation.[4] Using a single doxastic accessibility relation, with the identity of the believer and time of belief in the relata, not only allows for the representation of essentially self-locating beliefs, but also facilitates the representation of the relationships between the belief states of different believers (what they agree and disagree about, and what one may believe about another's beliefs), as well as the ways the beliefs of a single believer change over time.

So far, we have addressed only question (1), about the representation of a belief state as a whole. But when we come to question (2) (what is the content ascribed when one ascribes a particular belief?), the answer will be an ordinary proposition,

---

[4] See the appendix to this chapter for a little more detail about the formal model.

represented by a set of uncentered possible worlds. What makes it possible to describe belief states unambiguously by ascribing propositional belief is the assumption, mentioned above, that belief about where one is in the world is always also belief about what world one is in. This is the main substantive difference between the kind of model of self-locating belief that I am proposing and the Lewisian models, and it requires some explanation and defense. I need to explain, first, why it is reasonable to make this assumption, and second, what the benefits are of making it.

There are lots of realistic cases of self-locating ignorance or error, but all of them will be cases in which the subject's specific epistemic situation is unique in the actual world. Even though Alice didn't know, at noon, that it was then noon, it seems reasonable to believe that she never was, and never again will be, in *exactly* the epistemic situation that she is in then, with exactly the same experiences and memories that she was having at that time. And it is also reasonable to assume that no other actual person will be in exactly that situation. But in some *unrealistic* cases that have figured prominently in the discussion of self-locating knowledge and belief, it is assumed that there is, within the (fictive) actual world a duplication of epistemic scenarios. Such cases are standardly represented by using two or more *actual* scenarios to model the epistemic alternatives for the subject or subjects. I want to argue that even in such artificial cases, this way of modeling the situation is unnecessary and misleading. I will consider two notorious cases: first, the two allegedly omniscient gods in Lewis's story, cited in the heading of this chapter; second, the case of Sleeping Beauty.

3. LEWIS'S TWO GODS

The two gods, Lewis tells us, are not exactly alike. "One lives on top of the tallest mountain and throws down manna. The other lives on top of the coldest mountain and throws down thunder-bolts." But they are in identical epistemic situations: "Neither one knows whether he lives on the tallest mountain or the coldest mountain, nor whether he throws down manna or thunderbolts."[5] Since the two gods are omniscient with respect to propositional knowledge, the epistemic possibilities that model their ignorance must be distinct centered worlds that are differently centered on the same possible worlds.

It is not obvious that the coherence of this story will survive close examination (can different agents perform different actions, without realizing, as they act, which one of them is the agent of which action?),[6] but set this problem aside. Assuming it is coherent, how is Lewis's story to be reconciled with the assumption I am

---

[5] Lewis (1979), 139.

[6] The best I can do to make sense of Lewis's story is to liken it to Daniel Dennett's predicament at a certain point in his marvelous memoir, "Where am I?" (Dennett (1978)). In Dennett's tale, a body, Fortinbras, is connected remotely to two functionally identical brains, Hubert and Yorick (one electronic and one a human brain that is floating in the proverbial vat). Both brains receive the same perceptual input from Fortinbras, by way of radio signals, though only one of them at a time is able to control him. But since the brains are perfectly synchronized, Fortinbras does what both of his potential controllers simultaneously decide that he shall do, and so it seems to each subject that its decisions are efficacious. Hubert and Yorick are each ignorant of which is controlling Fortinbras (and also of which is the human brain, and which the electronic one). Now suppose we modify Dennett's story by saying that both synchronized brains are under the illusion that they are controlling *two* bodies, one on the tallest mountain, and one on the coldest mountain, while in fact one brain is controlling just one of the bodies, and the other the other. Put each brain into the head of the body controlled by that brain. Instead of remote radio connections to send the same perceptual inputs to two brains, we assume that each has divine perceptual capacities to see everything at once, from no particular perspective. Both gods decide both to throw down manna from the tallest mountain and to throw down thunderbolts from the coldest mountain. Each god knows that one of his decisions is efficacious, while the other is causally inert, but neither knows which is which.

This may be a way to make sense of the story, but if our gods engage in speech, this may have strange consequences. The god on the tallest mountain might say truly, and with confidence, "I don't know which mountain I am on, but I am on the tallest mountain." What both gods simultaneously decide is that these words shall come out of the mouth of that god. Neither god knows whether what he is trying to say is true, but each knows that if he succeeds in saying it, it will be true. So a sincere and true Moore-paradoxical statement is possible in this unusual situation.

making, that ignorance about where one is in the world is always ignorance about what possible world is actual? I must say that there are two qualitatively indiscernible worlds, and that neither god knows which of them is actual. This is what Lewis calls the haecceitist response, and he rejects it, first, because he rejects the haecceitist metaphysics. (On Lewis's view, there cannot be distinct but qualitatively indiscernible possible worlds.) But he also denies that the response will work, even given the haecceitist metaphysics. Here is his argument: suppose we assume that there is a world V that is qualitatively indiscernible from the world W of the story, but with the roles of the two gods reversed. This assumption won't help, according to Lewis, since we can simply stipulate that the gods know which of these two worlds they are in, and this will still leave them ignorant about where they are in the world. "Let the god on the tallest mountain know that his is world W rather than V. Let him be omniscient about *all* propositions, not only the qualitative ones. How does this help? Never mind V, where he knows he doesn't live. There are still two different mountains in W where he might, for all he knows, be living."[7] Lewis is right, I think, that the haecceitist move does not eliminate the need to link the believer to the worlds compatible with his or her beliefs, and so does not, by itself, provide an account of the states of ignorance of the two gods. The links are necessary to say how the possible states of the world are being used to represent the epistemic situations of our two characters. But we cannot simply stipulate that the gods know, of a certain possible world, that it is the actual world without saying more about what form their cognitive situations take. Suppose we name the gods Castor and Pollux, Castor being the one who is on the tallest mountain in the actual world W, and on the coldest mountain in the counterfactual alternative, V. How do we inform Castor that it is *Castor* who lives on the tallest mountain (and so that the actual world is W)?

[7] Lewis (1979), 141.

If we use the name to tell him, he first must be told to whom the name "Castor" refers, and we might do this in either of two ways (or he himself might fix the reference of the name in either of two different ways): we might say: "Let 'Castor' be your name," and then tell him that Castor is the god on the tallest mountain. (Or he might say to himself, "I hereby dub myself 'Castor'", and we then tell him where Castor is located.) Alternatively, we (or he) might say: "Let 'Castor' be the name of the god on the tallest mountain." On the first alternative, we have resolved Castor's doubts about his location in the world. In the second, we have not, but this is because he does not know of Castor that "Castor" is his name, and so does not yet know whether the actual world is W or V (this is a case like Gareth Evans's case of Julius[8]).

The haecceitist move does raise delicate questions about the relation between metaphysical issues about the world as it is in itself and issues about a subject's perspective on the world, just the issues our model is designed to help clarify. We don't want to rest a metaphysical distinction solely on its utility for the representation of knowledge and belief. But I think the haecceitist move can be justified on metaphysical grounds. Aside from the representation of cognitive states, it seems plausible (or as plausible as things get in this fanciful story) that it might be a contingent fact that our two gods have the properties that distinguish them: a contingent fact that the god who is on the tallest mountain is on that mountain, rather than the coldest mountain, where the other god in fact is, and that the one throws down thunderbolts, rather than manna, etc. The two gods, it seems, might have interchanged their positions and roles. Or, if this is not metaphysically possible because there are facts, perhaps about the origins of each of the

---

[8] "Julius" is a proper name, stipulated to be the name of the inventor of the zip, whoever he or she might be. "Julius" is (by stipulation) a rigid designator, so the proposition that Julius invented the zip is contingent, but one may still know a priori (in virtue of the stipulation) that Julius invented the zip, if any one person did. "Julius" made its first appearance in Evans (1979). I discuss the case in Stalnaker (2001).

two gods that are essential to them, and known by both of the gods, it still seems plausible to say that there might have been other individuals playing just these roles, and this is enough to suggests that there might have been qualitatively indiscernible possible worlds.

Note that this discussion brings out that the issue about self-locating knowledge and belief is not as tightly connected to semantic issues about personal pronouns and demonstratives as is sometimes supposed. If our gods give themselves names, fixing the referents demonstratively, then they can express their knowledge and ignorance using sentences that are *semantically* context-independent. ("I know that I am Pollux," says Pollux, "but I still don't know, in a sense, who I am, since I don't know which mountain Pollux lives on.") The introduction of the names does make it possible for others to express the same propositions with the same words, but it does not essentially change the epistemic situation of the relevant subjects. And of course names generally are most often introduced demonstratively. As is emphasized in both Perry's discussions of reflexive content, and in my uses of the diagonalization strategy, to explain cases of ignorance of the truth of identity statements involving proper names, we need to bring in information, not just about the referent of the names, but also about the facts that connect those names to their referent.

4. SLEEPING BEAUTY

Second, let me consider a case involving temporal self-location in which an individual may (for all she knows) be in essentially the same epistemic situation at two different actual times. Here is the scenario: Sleeping Beauty is to be put to sleep on Sunday night after being told that she will be woken up either once or twice in the next two days, depending on the flip of a fair coin. If heads, she is woken up only once, on Monday, and if tails, she will be woken up on Monday and again on Tuesday, but only after being given a drug that ensures that she will have no memory of the Monday waking. The question is, to what degree should Sleeping Beauty believe, upon being woken up on Monday, that the coin will, or did, land heads. Adam Elga, who introduced this puzzle to the philosophical literature,[9] defends the answer one third, while David Lewis argued that the rational degree of belief is one half.[10] The argument between Elga and Lewis is carried out within Lewis's centered-world framework for representing self-locating belief, and there are some presuppositions they share that I think should be questioned: they both assume that two of Sleeping Beauty's epistemic possibilities (when she wakes up on Monday) should be represented by two situations within the same possible world, and I think this assumption distorts the discussion. While I think Elga gets the right answer to the question posed by the puzzle, I want to use a slightly different argument to defend it.

Let's begin by describing Sleeping Beauty's epistemic situation when she wakes up on Monday. (Of course she does not then know it is Monday. We are describing the situation from the theorist's point of view.) There are three possibilities compatible with her knowledge at that point, which she would describe this way: "Either today is Monday, and the coin will land heads (call this state s1), or today is Monday and the coin will land tails (s2), or today is Tuesday, and the coin landed tails (s3)." Lewis and Elga both assume that (s2) and (s3) are alternative scenarios or predicaments within the same possible world. That is, they assume that the only fact about the world as it is in itself that is relevant is whether the coin lands heads or tails. Were Beauty to learn that fact, she would have all the relevant information about what possible world she was in; her remaining ignorance would be about where, within that world, she was. The first thing to note

---

[9] Elga (2000). As Elga notes, the problem has its source in a discussion in the game theory literature about games with imperfect recall.
[10] Lewis (2001).

about this way of modeling the situation is that it requires that Sleeping Beauty be in *precisely* the same epistemic situation on the two different days (on the assumption that the coin landed tails). It cannot be that it is slightly darker, or lighter, in the room in which she wakes up on one of the two days, or that the exact arrangement of the bedcovers that she sees as she wakes up is slightly different, or that she hears a dog bark in the distance on one day, but not the other. Sometimes a science fiction variant of the story is told in which an exact duplicate of Sleeping Beauty, as she was on Monday, is created on Tuesday, and while it does not seem essential to the problem posed by the story that it have this feature, it is essential to the way of modeling it used by both Elga and Lewis. But as the story is usually told, all that can be assumed is that she receive no information, on waking up on Monday (or Tuesday), that is *relevant* to the result of the coin toss, beyond the information that she wakes up, and we need only this weaker and more realistic stipulation if we assume that the epistemic alternatives are different possible worlds. (This assumption does not exclude the limiting case in which there are no differences, relevant or irrelevant, between Sleeping Beauty's situations at two actual times. "Even if the way things seem on the other day is *exactly* like this, down to the last detail," she might think (on both days), "it will still be not be *this* token experience that I was, or will be, having then.")

The account I am promoting says that the descriptions of the possibilities, (s1), (s2), and (s3), give the relevant information about three different possible worlds, viewed from a certain perspective. On this view, the perspective is essential to the *description* of the worlds, but not to the world-states described. In two of these possible states of the world ((s2) and (s3)), there is a similar event taking place either the day before or the day after the time that specifies the perspective, but the waking that will take place *tomorrow* (as Beauty would have put it at the time) in (s2) is a different waking from the one that is taking place *now* in (s3), and so scenario (s2) must be a different (uncentered) world from (s3). As we will see, this difference makes a difference to the argument.

There is a fourth possible state of the world that is *not* compatible with Sleeping Beauty's knowledge on Monday, but that she might describe, from her perspective, by means of two suppositions, one of which is counterfactual: "Suppose", she thinks, "that today is in fact Tuesday, but that instead of coming up tails, the coin had landed heads. I know that this is not the actual situation, because if it were, I would not have been woken up today, and I was." (Even if it is in fact Monday at the time Sleeping Beauty is thinking this particular thought, as we are supposing, she can still characterize this possibility as the one that is like the epistemically possible world in which (as she would put it) "Today is Tuesday", but in which the coin landed heads, instead of tails.)

The relevance of this fourth possible world to Sleeping Beauty's epistemic situation is that, while she is on Monday in a position to rule it out, she knows that on Sunday, she was not in position to rule it out. Of course on Sunday she was not in a position to characterize *any* of these possible situations by fixing the reference of the day in the way that she does fix it (on Monday) as *today*, or as the day in which *this* thought is being entertained. But we can still use these four possibilities to characterize Sleeping Beauty's prior state of knowledge, her epistemic situation on Sunday, doing it in a way that is relevant to connecting her knowledge on Sunday with her knowledge on Monday. Specifically, we can say what information it is that Sleeping Beauty acquires when she wakes up on Monday: what possibility that was previously compatible with her knowledge is now incompatible with it.[11]

Elga claimed that Sleeping Beauty received no new information upon waking up on Monday, and so that her rational change in belief (from one half to one third) in the proposition that the

[11] The point that Sleeping Beauty gains knowledge when she wakes up is argued in Weintraub (2004) and Horgan (2004).

coin would land heads, was a change induced by something other than new information. Elga claimed this because he identified new information with *objective* information, and in the centered-worlds framework that he was using, Sleeping Beauty learns nothing about what the world is like in itself. Elga's assumption that there could be rational belief change without new information was the main reason that David Lewis resisted his conclusion. According to Lewis, since Sleeping Beauty receives no new information, her degree of belief in heads must remain the same. But on the analysis I am proposing, one can agree with Lewis that new information is required for a rational belief change, but also with Elga that Sleeping Beauty's degree of belief in the result of the coin flip should change when she wakes up.

But does Sleeping Beauty really learn something—does she really rule out a possibility previously compatible with her knowledge—simply by being woken up on Monday (something she knew in advance would happen)? Suppose her best friend, Sleeping Ugly, accompanied Beauty on her adventure. He, let us suppose, will be woken up, put to sleep, and given the same amnesia inducing drug as Sleeping Beauty, but Sleeping Ugly will be awakened on Tuesday as well as Monday, whatever happens with the coin (and he will observe, each time, whether or not she is awakened). Surely Sleeping Ugly learns something upon waking up on Monday: he learns that Sleeping Beauty was also awakened. Does he learn anything that she does not learn? If we allow him to tell her what he has learned, is there anything he can tell her, when they both wake up, that she does not already know? Obviously not.

On the analysis I am promoting, the strategy for determining exactly what Sleeping Beauty's degrees of belief should be, when she wakes up, is to start by determining how her degrees of belief should be apportioned *on Sunday* between the possibilities that are open to her at that time. All parties to the dispute should be able to agree about this. Then her degrees of belief on Monday (and/or

Tuesday) will be determined simply by conditionalizing on the information that she receives on waking up. What is required for this strategy to work is that the possibilities that are relevant to representing her beliefs on Monday be a subset of those that represent her beliefs on Sunday, or more generally, that one be able to *calibrate* the informational states that she is in at the different times by characterizing them as subsets of the same set of possibilities. The unreconstructed Hintikka-style models of cognitive states took calibration for granted, but ignored belief change and self-location. The Lewis centered-worlds models recognized self-location, but provided no resources for representing the relations between informational states across time and across persons, and so no resources for clarifying the dynamics of knowledge and belief, or the communication of information between different subjects. The general framework that I am promoting allows for calibration across time, and across different subjects, but it also recognizes that calibration is a nontrivial problem, and may not be well defined in all cases.

5. COMPARING BELIEFS OVER TIME, AND BETWEEN DIFFERENT SUBJECTS

Sleeping Beauty remembers, on Monday, what she knew on Sunday, and that she knew it. We can represent this fact in a straightforward way by taking the possibilities compatible with her knowledge (on Monday) as full possible worlds, worlds in which she was in one cognitive state on Sunday, and another one on Monday. The information that she had at the earlier time can be preserved at the later time even if it was self-locating information. And by using the same possible worlds to represent the informational states of different subjects, we can say when they agree and disagree, even about self-locating information, and we can represent iterated attitudes—what one person believes about the beliefs of another person. Lingens the amnesiac,[12] for example, can consider, not only who he might be, but also what others might know or believe about who he is, and others may have beliefs about what Lingens does and does not know about his identity. To compare the information, including self-locating information, that is available to different subjects, and to represent what they know and believe about each other, we (as theorists) need to use the same possible worlds to model the various informational states, and the different ways in which we, and they, locate themselves in those possible worlds.

Since different subjects inevitably have different beliefs, and each has different beliefs at different times, comparisons of the contents of informational states across persons and times may require that subjects locate themselves in possible worlds that are not compatible with their present states of knowledge or belief. Self-locating information can *exclude* a certain possibility only if the subject locates herself in the situation that is excluded. Self-location in a counterfactual possible world was essential to the account of the Sleeping Beauty case, where she excluded (on Monday) the possible world in which it was *then* Tuesday, and the coin landed heads. Or consider Lingens, who has been doing research in the Stanford Library on various missing persons who he thinks he might be. "I still don't know who I am," he thinks, "but I know that I can't be Gustav Lauben, since if I were, I would have a tattoo of a mermaid on my right arm, and I don't." Here he locates himself in a counterfactual world, and as a result excludes it. Perhaps it was Daniels who suggested that he look into the Lauben possibility. "Daniels thought that I might be Lauben," thinks Lingens. Here he locates himself in a world that is compatible with what he takes Daniels's beliefs to be, but that is not compatible with his own beliefs.

[12] Rudolf Lingens made his debut in the philosophical literature in Frege (1919/1956). He first appeared in the role of an amnesiac lost in the Stanford library in Perry (1977).

Daniels, like Lingens, has read about Lingens, and just as Lingens does not know whether he himself is Lingens, Daniels doesn't know whether the famous Stanford amnesiac, the guy he has recently been talking to, the guy he thought might have been Lauben, *that* guy (as he might put it to himself, recalling the conversation), is Lingens. Lingens's ignorance of who he himself is is essentially self-locating, but Daniels has no problem with self-location. His ignorance about the identity of that guy is more like a standard Frege case, for example like Ralph's ignorance about Ortcutt in Quine's example—his failure to know that the pillar of the community that he sees on the beach and the suspicious man in the brown hat, glimpsed in the bar, are one and the same person.[13] Nevertheless, it seems that what Lingens doesn't know (that he is Lingens) is the same fact as the fact that Daniels doesn't know. If Daniels found out who the famous Stanford amnesiac was, he could tell Lingens in a straightforward way: When he says to him, "you are Rudolf Lingens" his "you" picks out, in each of the relevant possible worlds, the same person picked out by "I" in the mouth of Lingens (and the person that both pronouns pick out will be, in the possible worlds that this statement excludes, someone other than Lingens). We can capture this identity of content by representing their separate informational states, and their attitudes about each other, with the same possible worlds in which each locates himself and the other.

In cases of ignorance or confusion about identity (as in the case of Ralph and Ortcutt), it is not always clear where a subject should locate himself in the possible worlds compatible with the beliefs of someone else. Suppose Ortcutt knows about Ralph's confusions about him. Would he be correctly describing the situation if he said "Ralph believes that I am a spy?" In the world as Ralph takes it to be (and as Ortcutt takes Ralph to take it to be), should Ortcutt

[13] Quine (1956).

identify himself as the man on the beach, or as the distinct man in the brown hat in the bar? Ortcutt's problem here is the same as ours when we ask whether Ralph believes the singular proposition, about Ortcutt, that he is a spy. The right answer, I think, for both Ortcutt and for us, is that the attribution of that belief is correct in some contexts, but not in others.[14] But if we imagine a context in which Ralph and Ortcutt are discussing the situation, face to face, the answer will be clear. If the conversation takes place on the beach, with Ralph taking himself to be talking to the pillar of the community, who is not a spy, then it will clear that this is where Ortcutt locates himself in the world according to Ralph. He could sincerely say to Ralph, "you don't think I am a spy", and his statement would be unambiguously true.[15]

We can model a *conversational context* by a set of possible worlds that represents the common ground of the participants in the conversation—the information that they take to be shared between them. Like common knowledge, or mutual belief, common ground is an infinitely iterated attitude: roughly, a proposition is common ground in a group if each accepts it, each accepts that each accepts it, each accepts that each accepts that each accepts it, etc.[16] Since our models of self-locating belief can represent iterated belief, this kind of model of a context can accommodate self-locating communication. So long as the participants have a common way of identifying each other (as participants in the conversation), the iteration involved in defining the common

[14] Given our general framework, this means that it is right in some contexts to represent Ralph's beliefs with a set of possible worlds in all of which Ortcutt is a spy, while in other contexts it is wrong to use this set of possible worlds to represent his beliefs. See Stalnaker (1988) and Stalnaker (2008) for discussions of the context-dependence of de re belief ascriptions.

[15] Though if we tweak the context a bit, we could make it possible for Ortcutt also to say "you don't realize it, but you know me under a different guise, not realizing that that person is me. In that guise, you think I am a spy." Cf. Crimmins (1992).

[16] See Stalnaker (2002) for a discussion of this representation of context, though the issues about self-location are ignored in that discussion.

ground will give rise to a model of an informational state with a set of centered worlds with multiple individuals—all of the participants in the conversation—at the centers.[17]

The occasion for this digression on the general problem of self-locating attitudes was the suggestion that knowledge of the phenomenal character of experience was in some way like knowledge of who and where we are in the world, and that the problem posed by Mary's predicament might be solved by clarifying the analogy. We will return, in the next chapter, to the puzzle about Mary, exploring this analogy in the context of our general framework. In later chapters, we will use this framework to try to throw light on puzzles about a subject's knowledge of the contents of his or her own thought.

---

[17] See the appendix to this chapter for a few more details.

Appendix: Notes on models of self-locating belief

This is a brief sketch of a few details of a formal model, with a little motivation and commentary. The models use exactly the same abstract objects used in David Lewis's theory of de se belief (centered worlds), to characterize belief states, but uses them in a somewhat different way.

A model is a sextuple $<W, S, T, \geq E, R>$ where

1. W is a nonempty set of possible worlds
2. S is a set of *subjects* or believers
3. T is a set of times
4. $\geq$ is a binary transitive connected anti-symmetric relation on T, a relation that determines a linear order of the times.

T would most naturally have the structure of the points on the real line, but in simple models, we might choose to represent only the beliefs of our subjects at certain selected times, so the linear time order might be discrete, and the number of times might be finite. But it is assumed that the ordering is an objective time ordering, and that times can be identified across possible worlds. That is, a certain date (such as Tuesday, April 3, 2007) might be the date on which it rained in Oxford in certain possible worlds, and was sunny there in others.

Two definitions, before characterizing E and R:

    a. A *center* is a pair, $<A,t>$, where $A \in S$ and $t \in T$.
    b. A *centered world* is a pair $<c, w>$, where c is a center and $w \in W$.

5. E is the set of centered worlds meeting the condition that the subject of the center exists in the world at the time of the center.
6. R is a binary relation on E that is transitive, Euclidean and serial. R must also satisfy an additional condition, which we will state and explain below.

The interpretation of the fifth and sixth elements, E and R, is this: subjects may exist at some times at some worlds, and not at others. The set E of centered worlds is restricted to those that are relevant to representing a subject's beliefs at a time in a world. The relation R is the doxastic accessibility relation. To say that $<<A,t>, x>R<<B,t^*>, y>$ is to say that it is compatible with what A believes at time t in world x that she is in world y, that she is person B, and that the time is time t^*.

Given R, each centered world in E determines a set of centered worlds—those that are R-related to it. Call a pair consisting of a centered world and its R-related set a *belief state*, and call the determining centered world the *base (centered) world*, and the determined set the *belief set*. The role of the center of the base world is to specify the person whose beliefs are being represented, and the time at which she has those beliefs. The role of the centers of the centered worlds in the belief set is to represent where that subject takes herself to be in the world that, for all she believes, is actual. If Alice thinks, on Sunday, that it might be Monday, and that she might be Clara, rather than Alice, then a world centered on Clara on Monday will be compatible with what she believes (on Sunday).

We impose the following condition on the relation R:

(*) For any centers, c, c′ and c*, and worlds w and x: if $<c, w>$ $R <c′, x>$ and $<c, w> R <c^*, x>$, then $c′ = c^*$.

What this condition requires, intuitively, is that ignorance or uncertainty about where one is in the world is always also ignorance or uncertainty about what world one is in. Even in the highly artificial case where a subject believes that he will, in the actual world, be in two qualitatively indistinguishable situations at different times, t_1 and t_2, without knowing which time it is, it will remain true that (as he would put it at the time) the world where *this* token thought is occurring at time t_1 (and where another like it will occur at t_2) is a different (uncentered) possible world from the possible world in which *this* (token) thought is occurring at time t_2 (and another like it occurred at t_1).[1]

This crucial condition is the main point at which the proposed model differs formally from Lewis's account of de se belief, which allows that a case of ignorance might be represented by two centered worlds—two "predicaments", to use Adam Elga's term—centered at different points

---

[1] I don't want to rest anything on the assumption that the same token thought might have occurred on a different day. It might be a counterpart token that occurred, in the other possible world, on the other day. What one needs to motivate the assumption that there are two (uncentered) possible worlds here is just that the thought that takes place, in the actual world, at the other time is a different token thought.

within the same world. By requiring that ignorance and doubt always be represented by distinctions between possible states of the world, we allow for the calibration of the states of belief of different believers, and of a believer at different times. Even though belief *states* are represented by sets of centered possible worlds, the *contents* of belief can be taken to be ordinary propositions—sets of uncentered possible worlds. So in the interpretation of statements of the form "x believes that ϕ", the "that ϕ" will denote a set of (uncentered) possible worlds, even though the centers determined by a particular belief state may play a role in determining which proposition is denoted by a that-clause with indexical expressions in it. By taking the contents of belief to be (uncentered) propositions, we can straightforwardly compare the beliefs of different subjects, and we can model the way assertions change the context in a straightforward way. We can also model the dynamics of belief for a single agent—the facts about preservation and change of belief—in a straightforward way. In particular, we can apply a standard belief revision theory to a rational subject with a prior belief state at time t, who then receives some new information at time t* while remembering her prior state. Even if some of her prior and posterior information is self-locating (suppose, for example, she didn't know what time it was at t, or how much time passed between t and t*), she can still revise her beliefs in the standard way. If we want to add to our model probability measures on belief states to represent degrees of belief, this will be as straightforward as in standard belief logic models, and we could then represent the assumption that rational subjects will revise by conditionalization.

In the standard Hintikka-style semantics for logics of knowledge and belief, ordinary uncentered possible worlds are the relata of the doxastic or epistemic accessibility relations. The identity of the believer, and (implicitly) the time of belief are built into the relation. In a theory of this standard kind with multiple believers, there will be multiple accessibility relations, one for each believer. Our models, in contrast, need only a single doxastic accessibility relation, since the identity of the believer and the time of the belief are determined by the center of the first relatum. By putting the believer and the time of belief into the relata, rather than the relation, we not only provide the resources to represent self-locating belief, but also a more flexible framework for representing the relations between the beliefs of different believers, and of a single believer at different times.

In the standard belief semantics, the representation of iterated belief is a simple matter: If A and B are two believers, and R_A and R_B are their doxastic accessibility relations, then it will be true, in world w, that A believes that B believes that ϕ iff for all worlds x such that wR_Ax and all worlds y such that xR_By, ϕ is true in y. One can define the set of possibilities compatible with the *common beliefs* of A and B in terms of the transitive closure of the two relations R_A and R_B, or more generally, the common beliefs of a set of subjects in terms of the transitive closure of the set of accessibility relations for the subjects in the set. In our models, the representation of iterated belief is a little more complicated, but the complications reflect complexities in the phenomena being modeled, and the increased flexibility in the representational resources of the model. The first complication comes from the fact that we have made explicit that belief is relative to time, something that is ignored in the standard theory. One might represent A's beliefs at t about what B believes at some different time t′, but let's ignore that for now, and just focus on A's beliefs at some time t about what B believes at the same time. Still, A may not know what time it is, so the actual time at which A has her beliefs may be different from the time she takes it to be. For example, if A mistakenly believes on Tuesday that it is Monday, then there will be a difference between "A believes (on Tuesday) that B *now* believes that ϕ" and "A believes (on Tuesday) that B believes *on Tuesday* that ϕ." The truth of the former will depend on what B believes *on Monday* in the worlds compatible with A's beliefs, while the latter will depend on what B believes *on Tuesday* in those same worlds.

A second complication is this: Because of the intentionality of belief, A may have different beliefs about B's beliefs, relative to different ways of thinking about him. Suppose I am sitting in the bar with a man in a brown hat who is in fact Ortcutt, but I am not sure whether he is Ortcutt or O'Leary. We are watching the Red Sox on the television, and I believe that the man in the brown hat believes that the Red Sox are losing, since they *are* losing, and it is evident that the man is paying attention to the game. But I am not sure whether *Ortcutt* believes this, since for all I know, the man at the bar is O'Leary, and Ortcutt is somewhere else, blissfully ignorant of the state of the game.

In the simple case, where it is assumed that A knows who B is, we can ignore this, but for the general case, we need to relativize iterated belief, (what A believes about what B believes), to a way that A thinks of B (dare I call it a mode of presentation?), formally represented by a function from worlds to individuals. A function of this kind will represent (in a given world) a possible way of thinking *about B* if it takes B as its value in that world. In the simple case (where A knows who B is), this function will be the constant function, taking B for all arguments, but in the general case, it might be a variable, or non-rigid, individual concept. (We can assume that the function is everywhere defined within the worlds in A's belief set, since we can assume that if A identifies B as "the F", then A believes that there is a unique F.)

To use nonrigid functions, or individual concepts, to characterize the centered worlds does not add any new centered worlds to our model: it just gives us new ways to generalize about them. Suppose f is the non-rigid function, or individual concept, expressed by "the man in the brown hat", and that $f(w) = $ Ortcutt. Then the centered world $<<f, t>, w>$ is just the centered world $<<Ortcutt,t>, w>$. But when we quantify over centered worlds, f may take different values for different values of w. For example, consider this generalization:

For all worlds x and y and for all subjects C, if $<<A, t>, w> R$ $<<A, t>, x>$, and $<<f, t>, x> R <<C, t>, y>$, then $y \in \phi$.

This says that in world w, A believes that the man in the brown hat believes that ϕ.

Once we have a clear account of iterated belief, we can use it to define a notion of *common belief* for a group of individuals at a given time and the properties of a common belief state will be generated by the iterative process. It is common belief (among the members of group G) that ϕ iff all believe that ϕ, all believe that all believe that ϕ, all believe that all believe . . . , etc. To keep things simple, we might assume that everyone in the group knows who everyone else in the group is, but we can also model cases where the members of a group have some common way of identifying each other, even though they may not know who the others, or even themselves, are. So, for example, we might model the common ground (presumed common beliefs) of a conversation between two amnesiacs trying to figure out who and where they are, and what time it is, by pooling the meager information that they each have. In general, the common ground that is determined by the iterative process will generate a representation that parallels the representation of an individual belief state; it will have the same structure, but with centered worlds with multiple individuals at their centers. An individual belief state is a pair consisting of a centered world (the base world) and a set of centered worlds (the belief set). The common ground can also be represented by a base world and a common belief set, but with a sequence of individuals (all those in the relevant group) at the centers instead of a single individual. The sequences of individuals at the centers of the common belief worlds will represent where the members of the group mutually locate themselves and each other in the possible worlds compatible with their common beliefs.

Our models have an accessibility relation only for belief, but a subject might also have other self-locating attitudes. In some cases, self-location in possible worlds that are not compatible with the subject's belief is derivative from self-location in belief-worlds. (This fact was exploited in the account of the Sleeping Beauty case.) Suppose I don't know whether I am A or B, but I do know that if the coin had landed heads (which I know it did not), then I would have won the bet. What I know is that if I am in fact A, then if the coin had landed heads, A would have won, and if I am in fact B, then if the coin had landed heads B would have won the bet. A second kind of case of derivative self-location in worlds incompatible with the subject's beliefs is iterated belief. To represent my belief that John believes that I am a plumber, I need to locate myself in the possible worlds that, for all I believe, are compatible with what John believes. If John knows me in different guises (or if my beliefs about him allow for this possibility) then my self-location in the worlds as they are according to John will be relativized to one of them.[2]

[2] Thanks to Agustin Rayo and Seth Yalcin, both of whom gave me invaluable advice about the ideas developed in these notes.

4

Phenomenal and Epistemic Indistinguishability

In the pure phenomenal case, . . . the referent of the concept
is somehow present inside the concept's sense in a way that
is much stronger than in the usual case of direct reference.

David Chalmers[1]

My aim in this chapter is to explore the analogy between essentially
self-locating knowledge and knowledge of phenomenal experience,
but let me begin by reminding you where we are. The debates
about Mary and the knowledge argument raised questions about
the extent to which features of our representations of certain facts
(facts about phenomenal experience, "what it is like") belong to a
conception of the world as it is in itself (to what Bernard Williams
called an "absolute conception"). The alternative is that the distinctive facts about phenomenal experience should be understood
as features of our perspective on the world, facts that essentially involve the relation between a representation and something
being represented. Most of the materialist strategies for responding to the knowledge argument aim, in one way or another, to

---

[1] Chalmers (2003), 233.

explain the change in Mary's situation when she leaves her room and sees colors not as the learning of a new fact about the world as it is in itself, but rather some kind of change in her relation to the facts. The Fregean strategy aimed to do this by developing a more fine-grained notion of content that incorporated not just the truth conditions of what is said or thought, but also some elements of the way those truth conditions are presented to the thinker. The Lewis–Nemirow ability hypothesis aimed to explain the cognitive abilities that Mary acquires when she sees colors without invoking any notion of content. John Perry's strategy was to distinguish a special kind of content, *reflexive content*, which involved the relation between the representor and content in the ordinary sense: *subject matter content*. While I think it is right that the real issue underlying the puzzle is about representational content, and its relation to the representor, I suggested (in Chapter 2) that none of the standard approaches is sufficiently clear and explicit about exactly what content is, and about our cognitive relation to the contents of our thought. The aim of Chapter 3 was to develop a framework for getting clearer about these issues.

1. POSSIBLE WORLDS CONTENT AND THE ABSOLUTE CONCEPTION

There may be room for different conceptions of what it is that is said and thought, but the question raised by the knowledge argument is whether we need to refine our conception of the way the world is and the ways it might be in order to account for Mary's epistemic situation. To clarify this question, it helps to have *a* conception of informational content that can be abstracted from the relation to the representor, and that focuses exclusively on the demands that the correctness of the representation makes on the world. This is what the representation of content as a function from possible worlds to truth values tries to do.

David Lewis, in his admirable discussion of the case of Mary, uses this notion of content to spell out the consequences of accepting the conclusion of the knowledge argument—that Mary learns a distinctive kind of fact about the world as it is in itself. The conclusion is what he called "the hypothesis of phenomenal information":

> Besides physical information there is an irreducibly different kind of information to be had: phenomenal information. The two are independent. Two possible cases might be exactly alike physically, yet differ phenomenally. When we get physical information we narrow down the physical possibilities, and perhaps we narrow them down all the way to one, but we leave open a range of phenomenal possibilities.[2]

Lewis goes on to argue that the issue about this hypothesis is not really materialism or physicalism; he notes that no assumptions about the substance of a materialist or physicalist theory play a role in Jackson's argument. To bring this point out, Lewis invites us to suppose that some dualist theory is true: suppose there were spiritual fluids, or noetic forces, or irreducible, immaterial qualia, or whatever. Presumably we could write down a true theory about them (in black and white print), and let Mary read all about it. But this won't help her to know what it is like. The restriction that Jackson's thought experiment puts on Mary's education, Lewis persuasively argued, has nothing to do with the content of her information, but depends only on the form in which she receives it. So if the hypothesis of phenomenal information is correct, the upshot must be that this particular kind of information is for some reason incapable of being communicated.

I think Lewis is right that even a dualist should resist the hypothesis of phenomenal information, and I don't think talk of either modes of presentation, or of *concepts* will help to clarify the issues raised by the knowledge argument. But the strategy of developing an analogy with self-locating thought seems more

[2] Lewis (1988), 270.

promising, since the phenomena of self-locating thought can be represented in a way that makes explicit the relation between a conception of the world as it is in itself and a conception of the thinker's perspective on that world. The model of self-locating thought that I sketched in Chapter 3 aims to provide some resources for clarifying the complex relations between a perspective on the world and a representation of the world itself.

The model recognizes that any conception of the world is necessarily a conception that is formed from a certain place in the world, using the materials that are available then and there, but this fact does not prevent the conception from being an absolute conception, in the sense that its *content* is concerned exclusively with the way the world is in itself. One of the things that emerged from the discussion of examples of self-location is that there may be distinctions between the possibilities (the ways the world might be) that can be represented only from a certain perspective, but that once represented, can be abstracted from the perspective. On Monday (and Tuesday, should she be awake then), Sleeping Beauty was able to distinguish between a world in which, as she would put it then, *today* is Monday, and a different world in which *today* is Tuesday. On Sunday she was unable to distinguish between these two possible worlds, since in both of them an event of the same kind occurred on both Monday and Tuesday. To distinguish one from the other, one had to be there, or alternatively, to remember later having been there: one had to be in a position to refer uniquely to *that* particular time that Sleeping Beauty was awakened. But even on Sunday, Beauty was able to *describe* the distinction she was unable to make. Similarly, in our representation of Lewis's case of the two gods, we (viewing the worlds from outside) were able to *describe* a distinction between two qualitatively indiscernible possible worlds that could be distinguished from each other only from within one of the worlds.

One might be tempted to say that distinctions of this kind cannot be distinctions that are part of an absolute conception of the world, but I think this temptation rests on a conflation of questions about the content of a conception with questions about the possibility of forming a conception with that content. I take John Campbell to be conflating these two issues when he argues, in the context of a discussion of color, that "there is no 'absolute' or 'objective' conception which refers to particulars." His argument is that the world might contain qualitative duplicates, symmetrically arranged in a way that would make it impossible to distinguish different particular things, except by their relation to the one who is identifying them. Since the "defining feature of such a description of reality [an absolute description] is that understanding it does not require one to exploit anything idiosyncratic about one's own position in the world," this implies that the identification of particulars cannot be part of such a description.[3]

This seems to me confused. *Any* description, whether it refers to particulars or is in purely general terms, will necessarily involve a language, or some form of representation, and the representation will have the content it has in virtue of the position of the representor in the world; that is, in virtue of his, her or its relation to the particulars, kinds, properties and relations that the representation is about. But what is supposed to be absolute and objective, or not, is the content of the description, and not the means used to express that content. The fact that we cannot identify particulars except by using *our* names (which get their reference from *our* relations to the things) does not cast doubt on the objectivity of the propositions that we express. If it did, it would cast doubt on the objectivity of all representation.

I am not sure what consequences Campbell wanted to draw from his conclusion that "we have to abandon the notion of an 'absolute' or 'objective' description of reality which *identifies* particular things," but one may be tempted to take the conclusion to imply that our metaphysics must not allow distinctions between

---

[3] Campbell (1993), 179–80.

qualitatively indiscernible possibilities. Such a metaphysical conception might be defensible on other grounds, but I think it would be fallacious to defend it on the basis of facts about our capacity to refer. (Campbell does not himself draw this conclusion, and explicitly rejects the conclusion that particularity is mind-dependent.)

2. ESSENTIALLY CONTEXTUAL INFORMATION

It is true in general that what is said (self-locating or not) is said in a context, against a background of shared information that includes information about the context itself. Possible worlds compatible with the context—the shared background information—are possible worlds in which the participants in the conversation exist, and are having the conversation that they are having. This set of possibilities (linked to the participants for whom they are the live options) is the set of possible worlds that they intend to distinguish between with their speech acts. In making an assertion in such a context, one expresses a proposition (which might be represented by the set of possible worlds in which it is true), which, if it is accepted, changes the context by eliminating the possibilities in which it is false. In some cases, the links to the participants will be irrelevant to the information that is conveyed; that is, irrelevant to the way the possibilities are distinguished by the content of the speech act. Or, it may be that the links are relevant only as a means of determining the information the speaker intends to convey, and not to the information itself. (Suppose self-identification is not at issue—both of us know perfectly well who I am—but I use the first person pronoun to tell you that I was born in New Jersey. You take away from the conversation the objective information that Bob Stalnaker was born in New Jersey.) In such a case, we can detach the information from the context in which it was expressed, or from the situation in which it is believed. That is, we can identify the content of what is said or thought (the way it distinguishes between possible worlds) independently of the fact that it was something that was said or thought on that particular occasion. But sometimes, the information—the way a speech act or thought distinguishes between the possibilities that define the context—essentially involves the links. (It is information about the participants in the conversation as participants in the conversation, or about the subject of a belief, as the subject of that belief.) In such cases, the content cannot be detached from the context in which it is expressed or thought. In this kind of case, I will say that the information is *essentially contextual* information. So suppose you didn't know who I was, and what I told you was not that I was born in New Jersey, but that I was Bob Stalnaker. You would presumably learn *something* about the objective world from what I told you, together with what you already knew and what you observe, but there is not a piece of information that is the content of what I told you that you can simply add to your stock of beliefs about the objective world.

The point is not simply that a proposition can be about a context in which something is said, or about a person's location in the world. A piece of information about a speech act, or about a judgment or a belief can be an ordinary context-independent proposition that one might add to one's stable beliefs about the world. Consider, for example, the fact that David Kaplan said, or came to realize, on January 14, 1975 at 2:15 p.m. (p.s.t.), that his pants were on fire. Although this is a fact about a speech act, or occurrent thought that is essentially self-locating, the fact itself is not tied to any particular context in which it might be thought or expressed. The point about essentially contextual information is that sometimes the content of what is expressed or believed in a context is not detachable from the context in which it is expressed or believed. An example of John Perry's illustrates the point:

Suppose I am viewing the harbor from downtown Oakland; the bow and the stern of the aircraft carrier *Enterprise* are visible, though a large building obscures its middle. The name *"Enterprise"* is clearly visible on the bow, so when I tell the visitor "This is the *Enterprise*," pointing toward the bow, this is readily accepted. When I say, pointing to the stern clearly several city blocks from the bow, "That is the *Enterprise*," however, she refuses to believe me.[4]

The visitor refused to accept that *this* ship is the same as *that* one. This is a piece of contingent information that can be straight-forwardly represented as a distinction between possibilities that were open in the context of that conversation: the possible worlds excluded by the surprising information are those in which two different ships are visible on the two sides of the building. It is clear enough how to represent, in possible worlds terms, the increment of information—how the context, and the visitor's prior belief state would change if she accepted the information. But the context in which the possibilities are distinguished seems to be essential to the identity of the information. The day before, when the visitor was in a different place, she was not in a position to know, or to be ignorant of, this particular fact about the identity of the ships.

It seems intuitively right to say that the information that the visitor was given was not detachable from the situation in which she was given it, but can we say more explicitly what this comes to, in the context of our possible-worlds model? It is not that we cannot, from outside the context of the conversation with the visitor, describe the possibilities that the statement distinguishes between—the possibilities in which it is one ship on both sides of the building, and the possibilities in which there are two. But the information conveyed does not seem to be about the building; that is part of what is presupposed in the context. The model suggests that one should think of the acquisition or imparting of information in incremental terms. One begins in a prior belief state, or in a context represented by a set of possible situations, and the acquisition or expression of new information is constituted

---

[4] Perry (1977), 9.

by the elimination of some of those possibilities. In most cases, one eliminates possibilities in a context by coming to believe a proposition that distinguishes between a much wider range of possibilities, and that then becomes a more or less stable part of one's conception of what the world is like. But in some cases, what is said, or learned, distinguishes only between the possibilities in a local context. Linguists sometimes represent the meaning of a sentence as its *context change potential*: as a function taking a prior context into a posterior context.[5] This is a representation that is restricted to the minimal job that a piece of information is required to do. To the extent that it does no more, or little more, the information will be essentially contextual.[6]

Even when the proposition that is used to characterize a state of knowledge or a speech act is defined for a set of possible worlds that extends well beyond those in a given context set, the relevance of that proposition to the cognitive state of the subject, or to the intentions of the speaker, may be limited to a more or less local context. The cognitive capacity that a theorist or attributor is using a proposition to describe when he says what a subject knows is a capacity to distinguish between the members of a certain set of relevant alternative possibilities, and a proposition is apt for describing a subject's cognitive capacity, or the intentions of a speaker, provided that it captures the distinction that the subject has the capacity to make, even if in another context it would not. A variation on one of our examples will, I hope, make this abstract point clearer: Lingens the amnesiac, let us suppose, is not the only one who doesn't know who he is. In order to determine his

[5] See Heim (1983).

[6] There will be a continuum of cases, rather than a line between essentially contextual and context-independent information. And it is important to note that this distinction is not tied to the indexicality of the sentences used to express information. More robust and context-independent information may be expressed, in some contexts, with tenses and indexicals. The context-dependence may be entirely in the relation between what is said and the means used to say it. And essentially contextual information may be expressed with names (rather than pronouns) introduced in local context.

identity, his story is widely publicized, and is much discussed in the tabloid press. He is given a name, "Nathan", and there is a lot of speculation about who Nathan might be. One day, O'Leary and Daniels see an excited crowd of autograph seekers surrounding a celebrity emerging from a limousine. "Do you know who that is?" O'Leary asks Daniels. "Yes, that's Nathan, the Stanford amnesiac," Daniels replies. Was Daniels telling the truth when he said that he knew who that was? Is he in a position to have singular beliefs about Nathan (a.k.a. Lingens)? He has the capacity to distinguish possible worlds in which it is that person who is emerging from the limousine from situations in which some other celebrity is the one fending off the autograph seekers, and so we can correctly refer to Lingens himself to describe a set of possibilities that Daniels can distinguish between. But in another context, where what is in question is whether Nathan is Lingens or Lauben, we would need to describe Daniels's cognitive situation in terms of a set of possibilities that includes some in which "Nathan" refers to Lingens, and some in which that name refers to Lauben. Relative to such a context, we have to say that Daniels does not know who Nathan is.[7]

3. MARY AND THE ANALOGY WITH ESSENTIALLY CONTEXTUAL INFORMATION

Perhaps the way Mary changes upon leaving her room is by moving to a context in which the resources available to her for distinguishing between the possibilities change. Perhaps her new knowledge is essentially contextual in a way that is something like our knowledge of who and where we are in the world. I will

---

[7] See the paper by John Perry, and my response to it, in Byrne and Thomson (2007), for a discussion of a case involving self-location and context shifting.

first try to develop this analogy, and then look at a surprising consequence of taking it seriously, a consequence that will provide some intuitive grounds for resistance.

Start with a simple and unproblematic example of essentially contextual knowledge:

Alice, of the Homeland Security bomb squad, is in the Rose Garden on Tuesday morning, 10:47 a.m. She points to the ground beneath a particular rose bush, and says, "a bomb is buried there, and unless we defuse it *now* it will explode within five minutes."

Barry is in a room far away from the Rose Garden on Monday, and he knows that the next day, at 10:47 a.m. there will be a bomb buried under the rose bush which is 10.25 meters east and 4.35 meters north of the southwest corner of the garden (the very place that Alice will be pointing to), and that unless it is defused soon after that, it will explode before 10:52.

Barry knows a lot about the situation, in this little story, but he doesn't know what Alice will know the next day. He is not in a position to know this; he would have to be there. Is the knowledge that Mary lacks, in Jackson's story, something like this? It is knowledge that, after she gets it, is naturally expressed with a demonstrative ("Now I know that seeing red is like *this*"), and her relation to what she is demonstrating (the type of experience she is having or recalling) seems to be essential to the character of the information it is used to express in the way that it is in the case with Alice. But the analogy, if it implies that Mary is not ignorant of any relevant fact about the world as it is in itself, may seem strained. Before considering one reason why it might seem strained, let me sketch a variation on the story about Mary that I hope will make clearer exactly what the analogy is supposed to be.[8]

---

[8] I discuss this variation on the story in Stalnaker (2003b). Martine Nida-Rümelin's variation, mentioned in Ch. 2, makes a similar point, although she draws very different conclusions from it. Daniel Stoljar's case of experienced Mary in Stoljar (2005) is also relevant.

Suppose that Mary, still in her room, is told that she will be subjected to the following experiment. She will be shown either a red or a green star, to be chosen by the flip of a coin, and she is told in great detail the exact circumstances of the two possible scenarios. So given her extensive knowledge of neurophysiology and color science, she knows that when the experiment is performed, she will be in the presence of a star with one of two specific light reflectance properties, and will be in one of two specific brain states. Both before and after the experiment is performed, there are two possible worlds compatible with Mary's knowledge—call them worlds R and G. As it happens, the red star is chosen, so she is in fact in possible world R.

In a sense, after the experiment is performed, Mary knows what it is like to see red, although not under that description. "Now I know", Mary says, "either what it is like to see red, or what it is like to see green. I just don't know which it is, since for all I know, *this* experience could be the experience of seeing red, or of seeing green." (To use the terminology I introduced in Chapter 2 in discussing John Perry's response to the knowledge argument, this experiment takes Mary only to stage one of the cognitive achievement of learning what it is like to see red.)

What changed about Mary's epistemic situation when she was shown the star is that she was then in a position to represent information about *this* experience, just as Alice, at the scene of the impending explosion was in a position to represent, in her speech and her thought, the contextual information that *that* bomb is about to explode (that is, will explode soon after *now*). Note that Mary's situation is *not* being compared with the situation of amnesiacs or people who do not know what time it is, or where they are. Rather, the analogy is this: Mary is like Barry, who is not in a position to know a certain piece of contextual information because he is not in the relevant context. Mary's situation with respect to color (when she is still in her room) is like his situation with respect to Alice, whose warning about the bomb took place far away, and at a different time. Barry knew the relevant objective facts; there is no further information that we might have given to him, in his room on Monday, to bring it about that he knew what Alice knew. He would have had to be in Alice's situation—in her context—and to have known that *this* is the place (10.25 meters east, and 4.35 meters north from the southwest corner) and it is *now* 10:47.

If you buy this analogy, then you can explain the knowledge Mary lacks when she is still in her room, and you can understand that knowledge in terms of the elimination of possibilities, without invoking the hypothesis of phenomenal information that explains phenomenal information in terms of finer distinctions between the possibilities. But, the fans of qualia will protest, the analogy won't fly. There is nothing essentially indexical or demonstrative about the information Mary lacks. Let's assume she had, while still in her room, a name, "ph-red" for red-type qualitative experience. That is, "ph-red" is a name that designates a phenomenal experience type: the type of experience that people like Mary would have when looking at red things in normal conditions. Presumably, the property of being in a ph-red state is correlated with a physical/functional state type, and if materialism is true, then presumably that property *is* a physical/functional state type. Mary, because of her vast empirical knowledge, knew all about the physical/functional property that is or correlates with the property of being in a ph-red state, though she didn't know what it was like to be in a state of this type. Then, when she is shown the red star, she wonders whether *this* experience is ph-red. But Mary could then coin another name for her experience. Suppose, following John Perry, she names it "wow". Now she can express her question, initially posed with a demonstrative, whether *this* is ph-red as a question about a context-independent, objective proposition: is it true that wow = ph-red?

But note that the same kind of maneuver could be made in the Rose Garden bomb scenario. Barry, since he doesn't know what time it is when he arrives, says, "I hereby dub the time five minutes from now, 'pow'. I know the bomb will explode by 10:53 a.m., but will it explode at pow?''

But (the objector continues) the cases seem different in this way: when Barry named the time "pow" he didn't know what time he was naming, and so didn't know what objective proposition he was asking about. But when Mary saw the red star, and named her experience "wow", she knew what she was naming, since she was *acquainted* with the experience; she had acquired a *pure phenomenal concept* of it. But I want to question the assumption that there is something—phenomenal experience—that has both an autonomous place in a conception of the world as it is in itself and also this kind of distinctive epistemic role. I will conclude this chapter by looking at an intuitively attractive and widely shared assumption about the relation between knowledge and experience that I think is one of the sources of resistance to the strategy I am suggesting for defusing the knowledge argument.

4. THE PRINCIPLE OF PHENOMENAL INDISTINGUISHABILITY

The assumption, which I will call the principle of phenomenal indistinguishability, is this:

If a possibility is an epistemic alternative for a knower at a time (that is, it is compatible with his or her knowledge) then it is *phenomenally indistinguishable* from the actual world to the knower at that time.[9]

The notion of phenomenal distinguishability I have in mind is a simple epistemic capacity—the capacity that a subject may have to distinguish cases where she is in one or another of two types

---

[9] Thanks to Tim Williamson for pointing out a problem with an earlier formulation of this principle.

of experiential state.[10] Two experiential states of a person are phenomenally indistinguishable to the person just in case she can't tell the difference when she shifts from one to the other. Suppose, to take a standard kind of example, we have two quite different light reflectance properties that seem exactly the same color to a normal perceiver. One of the patterns of light is projected on a screen, and then replaced by the other. The viewer cannot tell when the transition takes place.

There would be lots of problems if one tried to pin down the notion of phenomenal indistinguishability precisely. Because our discriminatory capacities are limited, there will be intransitivities and borderline cases, and there may be issues about what to say when the subject's inability to discriminate is caused by extraneous factors (for example, when the subject is unable to pay sufficient attention). It will be particularly problematic to say exactly what it means for two highly complex visual scenes to be phenomenally indistinguishable. Consider, for example, the phenomenon of inattentional blindness, illustrated in experiments in which two pictures of a complex scene are alternated on a screen. The two pictures differ in a way that is perfectly obvious once pointed out (in one example, a large jet engine on an airplane is airbrushed out in one of the pictures), but before their attention is directed to it, subjects are often unable to find the difference, or to distinguish between the way the two pictures look.[11] Does this count as phenomenal indistinguishability? This will depend on exactly how experiential state types are individuated, and how one distinguishes a capacity from the exercise of it. I am not going to worry about these issues, since the counterexample to the principle that I want to consider involves

[10] See the Introduction to Byrne and Logue (forthcoming) for a discussion of phenomenal indistinguishability in the context of arguments for and against disjunctivist theories of perception.
[11] See Simons and Rensin (2005).

experiential states that are simple, and *obviously* discriminable, on any plausible way of pinning the notion down.

To say that two alternative (centered) possible worlds are phenomenally indistinguishable is to apply this notion counterfactually: if the subject who is in fact in one of the possible situations were, contrary to fact, to be shifted to a state of the type she is experiencing in the other, she wouldn't know the difference. So what the principle says is that if two possible situations are epistemic alternatives for a person, then they will be situations that the subject lacks this kind of capacity to distinguish. It may appear to be a truism that if two possible situations are epistemic alternatives—if one doesn't know which of them one is in—then one lacks the capacity to discriminate between them. But there may be a conflation of different notions of discrimination underlying this appearance.

The empiricist holds that the evidential basis for all our knowledge is experience—phenomenal experience. Whatever the right story to tell is about how our knowledge can get beyond our experience, it seems natural to assume that we at least can know that the quality of our immediate experience is the way that it in fact is. But our story about Mary in the coin flip scenario seems to conflict with this natural assumption.

Mary has just seen a red star, but is ignorant of whether it is red or green. The two possible situations we used to represent her ignorance were physically different: World R is the actual world, while in nonactual world G she is presented with a green star, with all the optical and physiological consequences that that would have had in the actual world. (Since Mary knows all the general optical and physiological facts, these facts will hold in all worlds that are epistemically possible for her.) But it seems intuitively that these two possible worlds are phenomenally as well as physically different. If the flip of the coin had been different, and Mary had been shown the green star instead, things would have looked very different to her. Nevertheless, she still doesn't know which of the two situations she is in.

If it is assumed that epistemic alternatives must be phenomenally indistinguishable, then world G cannot be compatible with Mary's knowledge. To account for Mary's ignorance of which color she has seen in this case, one will be required to suppose that there is a different possible world, G* which is *physically* just like the world G, but *phenomenally* just like the world R, and if we accept that, we have bought the hypothesis of phenomenal information.

Before looking at the upshot of rejecting the principle of phenomenal indistinguishability, let me take a quick look at what happened to Mary after the experiment I have described took place. She was not allowed out into the world, but confined again, this time into the Nida-Rümelin room (which, you will recall, is a room wallpapered with randomly colored shapes, but with no recognizable colored objects). This time Mary is accompanied by her friend, Pierre (about whom we will hear more in the next chapter), who at this time is still a monolingual speaker of French, a language Mary does not know. She never does learn which of the two colors it is that she has seen, but she experiences many other colors, not knowing which they are either. But Pierre teaches her the names of the colors, in French, by ostension. Perhaps she learns a lot of French from Pierre, not by translation into English (since he doesn't know English), but from the ground up. So she comes to know that the star she first saw was the color named "rouge" in French, but still does not know whether it is red or green (or at least whether it is the color called "red" or the color called "green"). (I know that it strains credibility to tell you that the brilliant Mary couldn't figure out which colors were which, after all this time, and with all this information, but we left realism behind a long time ago, in telling this story. I don't think the points I want to make with the help of this extension of it depend on it being realistic.) Should we still say, at this point, that Mary doesn't know what color things that she sees are? She knows of red things that they are rouge, and of rouge things that they give rise to the "wow" type phenomenal experience. Why does her old word "red" connect more directly to the property *red* than her new word "rouge"? (And why does her old word "ph-red" connect more or less directly to her phenomenal experience of red than her new word "wow"?) We, who attribute belief and knowledge, refer to properties and things (and qualia, if there are such things) and characterize the content of other people's belief in terms of those things. In the right context, we might use the property *red* to represent Mary's capacity to identify some object in her room as "rouge", even if in another context it would be right to say that she still does not know what color objects that look like that are. In particular, since she still lacks the ability to connect her prior theoretical knowledge of the property red, and of red experience to the knowledge she would express with the words "rouge" and "wow", in contexts where that ignorance is particularly salient, it may be appropriate to continue to say that Mary still does not know which colors she is experiencing.

Decades of discussion of Frege cases have got us used to the facts that things (and properties) can impact our cognitive lives in different ways, and that we may be unaware that it is one thing, rather than two, that we know about in two different ways. If I don't know that Hesperus is Phosphorus, does that mean that I don't know what Hesperus (or Phosphorus) is, or what "Hesperus" (or "Phosphorus") refers to? The notion of knowing what or who something or someone is is notoriously problematic, and context-dependent. Some have argued that we never really know, about things in the external world, what they are in themselves—never know what they are in what David Lewis calls "an uncommonly literal and demanding sense"[12]—but phenomenal experience was supposed to be different. It is presented directly; it is supposed to be its own mode of presentation.[13] Pure phenomenal concepts such as the ones that Mary allegedly acquires when she leaves her

----

[12] Lewis (1995), 327.   [13] Loar (1990).

room "characterize . . . the phenomenal quality as the phenomenal quality that it is".[14] David Chalmers, spelling out the special status of phenomenal concepts in the context of a two-dimensional possible worlds framework, says that they are both epistemically and subjunctively rigid, which seems to imply that we have direct epistemic access to the essential nature of the phenomenal property. But I am skeptical that there are things—pure phenomenal concepts—that have these mysterious properties, or that there is anything that will connect our knowledge to our experience in a way that vindicates the principle of phenomenal indistinguishability. Whether or not one shares this skepticism, my argument is that if we do buy that principle, we are stuck with the hypothesis of phenomenal information, with all of its problems. The bottom line is that *the principle of phenomenal indistinguishability, together with the facts about what Mary knows and does not know in the coin flip scenario, entail the hypothesis of phenomenal information.*

On the other hand, if we reject the principle, we are left without an intentional foundation, a point at which our thought meets its subject matter in a direct and context-independent way. Our epistemic relation to our experience is like our epistemic relation to anything else in the world. If this is right, then we should not think of our epistemic relation to Hesperus, or water, as indirect in a way that contrasts with some alternative epistemic relation. Perhaps there is no "uncommonly literal and demanding sense" in which we know things as they are in themselves. Perhaps our knowledge of the internal world is as indirect as our knowledge of what lies beyond it. Or more plausibly, perhaps we need a better conception of what it is for knowledge to be direct.

[14] Chalmers (2003), 233.

5

Acquaintance and Essence

> Every proposition which we can understand must be com-
> posed wholly of constituents with which we are acquainted.
>
> Bertrand Russell[1]

Saul Kripke's story about Pierre is as notorious as Frank Jackson's
story about Mary. I am going to start this chapter with Kripke's
story, and the lesson that David Lewis thought we should draw
from it about what Pierre does and does not believe. Then I
will connect this lesson with Lewis's views about what we do
and do not know and believe about the qualitative character of
experience. I will discuss a number of interconnected theses that
Lewis discusses: about our relation to the contents of our thought,
about the way a materialist should understand qualia, and about
the role of phenomenal experience as a foundation for knowledge.
There are conflicts between these theses that I will argue derive
from a mix between internalist and externalist perspectives, and
that I think help to bring to the surface some assumptions that
underlie the puzzles about our knowledge of our own states of
mind. I will suggest that we need a more thoroughgoing externalist
perspective, and a more thoroughgoing contextualism than Lewis

---

[1] Russell (1917/1957).

defends in order to get clear about our knowledge of experience and thought. There will remain some familiar tensions between externalism about content and our special access to content, which I will focus on in the next chapter.

1. PIERRE AND SINGULAR THOUGHT

Pierre, you recall, was this monolingual French speaker who learned about the famous far away city London (though he called it "Londres"), and came to believe that London is pretty. Later, he moved to London, learned English, and came to believe that London is not pretty. But since he didn't realize that the city he moved to was the same city he had learned about earlier, he continued to hold his original belief, continuing to say, when speaking French, "Londres est jolie."

David Lewis took the story to be a decisive refutation of "a certain simple analysis of belief sentences," an analysis that he argued "fails for another reason as well, since it requires believers to have a knowledge of essences which they do not in fact possess."[2]

The simple analysis in question is the analysis that says that the content of Pierre's belief that London is pretty is the singular proposition that says, of London, that it is pretty—the proposition that is true in possible worlds in which that city is pretty, and false in possible worlds in which it is not. The analysis is refuted, Lewis argued, because it yields the conclusion that Pierre, according to the story, has contradictory beliefs. But Lewis agrees with Kripke that this conclusion is unacceptable. Pierre "lacks information, not logical acumen. . . . He cannot be convicted of inconsistency: to do so would be incorrect."[3]

But Lewis argued that we shouldn't need a case where the subject thinks of a thing in two different guises to see the

---

[2] Lewis (1981), 408.   [3] Lewis (1981), 409, quoting Kripke (1979).

inadequacy of the singular proposition analysis. We should reject it even in an ordinary case where the believer has just one way of thinking about London, or George W. Bush, or the Eiffel Tower. The problem, he argues, is that to attribute a singular belief about an object to someone is to attribute knowledge of the essence of the object to the believer, knowledge that the believer rarely or never has. Lewis made the point by describing a possible world that (he claims) "fits Pierre's beliefs perfectly," but in which a city distinct from London plays the role that London in fact plays. That is, he argues that there is a possible world compatible with Pierre's beliefs in which a different city (Bristol, as it happens) acquires the name "Londres" (in French) and is the origin of the beliefs that Pierre expresses, in that world, by saying "Londres est jolie." The counterfactual world that Lewis describes has Pierre in it, and Pierre's perspective in that world is exactly the same as it is in the actual world: things seem to Pierre exactly as they actually seem, "from the inside". The reason we are able to describe a possible world in which Pierre's word "Londres" refers to a city different from London is that (all agree) Pierre is ignorant of some of the essential properties of London, which implies that there will be possible worlds compatible with Pierre's knowledge in which the city in question lacks some of those properties, and so is not our London. It seems reasonable in any case, from an intuitive point of view, to say that such possible worlds are compatible with Pierre's beliefs, since were a world of this kind to have turned out to be actual, Pierre would have said that things turned out exactly as he expected. And this argument does not depend on the distinctive feature of Pierre's situation—that he knows London in two different ways. For any of us who is ignorant of some of the essential properties of some city, person or thing e, one could describe a counterfactual world in which a different city, person or thing played the role that e actually plays, but which otherwise answers to the subject's conception of what the world is like.

There is a straightforward objection to this argument, which Lewis anticipated: the objection simply denies that the counter-example world is one that fits Pierre's beliefs. "For Pierre believes that London is pretty," the objector says, "whereas the counter-example world is one where London is not pretty." The objector grants that Pierre, in Lewis's counterexample world, will say that things turned out exactly as he expected, and he acknowledges that Pierre will be right, in that world, since what Pierre believes in *that* possible world is different from what he believes in the actual world. But (the objection continues) this does not imply that what Pierre *actually* believes is true in that possible world. The dialectic is familiar from the arguments about Twin Earth, and from Tyler Burge's defenses of anti-individualism. The anti-individualist agrees that things are internally the same for Pierre in the counterfactual world as they are in the actual world when he says or thinks, "Londres est jolie", but argues that this does not imply that the content of his statement or thought is the same. But Lewis and the internalists argue that unless we take a belief to be "an inner, narrowly psychological state," we cannot account for a believer's access to his own beliefs. If we take the content of Pierre's belief to be a singular proposition, then we must say that Pierre has contradictory beliefs. "Anyone is in principle in a position to notice and correct a state of the head which can be characterized by assigning contradictory propositional objects, but why should philosophical and logical acumen help him if the trouble lies partly outside? As soon as we accept the consistency of Pierre's beliefs as a datum—as I did, on Kripke's invitation—we are committed to the narrowly psychological conception of belief and its objects."[4]

I think Lewis is wrong about two things here: first, that we need a narrowly psychological conception of intentional states in order to explain the way in which Pierre is consistent, and more generally to account for the kind of knowledge of his attitudes and reasoning

[4] Lewis (1981), 416.

that he has. But second, I also think that it is less clear than Lewis supposes that our access to our intentional states would be unproblematic if we assumed that they were intrinsic states of the head. The qualitative properties of our experience are presumably narrowly psychological in the sense Lewis has in mind, and yet our knowledge of them is not unproblematic, as we have seen. Lewis, at least, argues that we don't know their essences any more than Pierre knows the essence of London. I will look at Lewis's somewhat equivocal account of qualitative experience and our knowledge of it, before turning, in the next chapter, to the challenge of reconciling an anti-individualist account of propositional content with the kind of knowledge of it that thinkers must have if we are to account for their rationality.

2. THE IDENTIFICATION THESIS

Just as Lewis thinks that we cannot have singular beliefs about a particular city or person without knowledge of the essence of the city or person, so he thinks that we cannot have singular beliefs about the qualitative character of our experience without knowing the properties that are essential to them. One might conclude that since we obviously are acquainted with the character of our experience, we thereby must know their essential nature, and Lewis thinks that it is part of the folk concept of phenomenal experience that we do have such knowledge, simply in virtue of having the experience. But he argues that this is a mistake—a part of the folk concept that we should reject. That is, we should reject what Lewis calls "the identification thesis" which is the thesis that "the knowledge I gain by having an experience with quale Q enables me to know what Q is—identifies Q—in this sense: any possibility not ruled out by the content of my knowledge is one in which it is Q, and not any other property instead, that is the quale of my experience. Equivalently, when I have an experience with quale Q, the knowledge I thereby gain reveals the essence of Q: a property of Q such that, necessarily, Q has it and nothing else does."[5]

The Identification Thesis, as Lewis understands it, is like the revelation thesis that some philosophers take to be part of our folk concept of color.[6] This thesis holds that there can be nothing in the nature of a color property that is not fully revealed in the visual experience of color. Analogously, the Identification Thesis requires that there can be nothing to the nature of a phenomenal experience that is not revealed to one who has the experience. It is clear that a materialist like Lewis who is committed to the thesis that qualia are physical properties of physical events must reject this thesis, since having an experience does not reveal the specific physical nature that, according to the materialist, they essentially have.

I think Lewis is right to reject the Identification Thesis, but I also think the consequences of doing so are more radical than he realized. It is one thing to conclude, as Lewis does in his discussion of Pierre, that our knowledge of things like cities and people is indirect, mediated by knowledge of the contingent properties of those things. But if knowledge of the character of phenomenal experience is indirect in the same way, what is it mediated by? Lewis himself assumed that experience plays a special role in providing a foundation for knowledge, and his account of this role conflicts with his rejection of the Identification Thesis.

3. LEWIS'S ANALYSIS OF KNOWLEDGE

What we know, on Lewis's account of knowledge, is what is true in all of the possibilities that are unelimated by our evidence, and

---

[5] Lewis (1995), 328.
[6] See Johnston (1992) and Jackson (1998) for discussions of the revelation thesis.

the *evidence* that does the eliminating is identified with experience. Lewis gave a characteristically sharp and clear formulation of what it means for a possibility to be eliminated by evidence:

I say that the uneliminated possibilities are those in which the subject's entire perceptual experience and memory are just as they actually are.... A possibility *W* is *uneliminated* iff the subject's perceptual experience and memory in *W* exactly match his perceptual experience and memory in actuality.[7]

Lewis, in the context in which he gave this definition, is mainly concerned with the problem of how, if knowledge is understood in terms of the elimination of possibilities by experience, we are able to answer the skeptic. His strategy for reconciling the thesis that knowledge requires the elimination of possibilities by experience with the possibility of knowledge that goes beyond experience was to give a contextualist account of knowledge that permits us, in context, to ignore certain possibilities that are *not* eliminated by experience. But on Lewis's account, we will at least know, *in any context*, that the possibilities excluded by our experience—possible situations in which our experience does not match our actual experience—are possibilities that are incompatible with our knowledge. The problem is that all of these possibilities will be possibilities in which our experience has whatever essential properties our actual experience has. That is, Lewis's account of knowledge implies that even in the most skeptical context, we will know the essential nature of our experiences—"know exactly what they are ... in an uncommonly demanding and literal sense of 'knowing what'." This means that Lewis's account of knowledge entails the Identification Thesis that he rejects, and it also entails the principle I discussed at the end of the last chapter—that epistemic alternatives must be phenomenally indistinguishable. And as we noted there, this

[7] Lewis (1996), 424.

principle commits us to the hypothesis of phenomenal information, which Lewis argued so effectively against.[8]

The source of the tension in Lewis's account, I think, is that it is motivated by a mix of internalist and externalist ideas. The reason experience and memory are given a special and context-independent role in determining what the subject knows is that they are supposed to be accessible from the inside and independent of what lies outside. That is the internalist idea. But Lewis's account of the elimination of possibilities is resolutely externalist in that the evidence that gives knowledge is described from an external point of view. In this respect, his account of the role of experience in providing a foundation for knowledge is like the view of Quine and Sellars, discussed in Chapter 1. Lewis insisted that it is not the propositional content of our experience that does the eliminating. "Rather, it is the existence of the experience." World W is eliminated, not because the experience *represents* the world as being different from W, but because W is a world in which the subject is not having the experience. Lewis says that his account does not require him "to tell some fishy story of how the experience has some sort of infallible, ineffable, purely phenomenal propositional content ... Who needs that?"[9] But Lewis is stuck with infallibly known evidence propositions whether he wants them or not, since there is (on his account) a proposition that is true in exactly those possible worlds in which the subject's experiences exactly match his experiences in the actual world, and this proposition corresponds to a fact that the subject knows, simply in virtue of having the experiences that he in fact has.

---

[8] Cf. Hawthorne (2004), 60, n. 26: "Lewis's account ... directly secures the thesis that we automatically know any fact that supervenes on our evidence (where for Lewis, 'evidence' means the intrinsic facts pertaining to one's experience and memory). This is very odd: If I have a visual array with 137 phenomenal red dots, it would not seem that I automatically know that."

[9] Lewis (1996), 424–5. The three dots are in the text, and not an ellipsis.

I think Lewis's account of knowledge is right to represent knowledge in terms of a set of unelimated possible situations. We won't have an adequate account of knowledge if it does not connect a state of knowledge with the way the world is, according to the knower. The problem is that the account does not recognize the extent to which knowledge claims are contrastive and context-dependent. Lewis's account is a contextualist one, allowing that certain possibilities (determined by context) that are not eliminated by experience are nevertheless properly ignored. But what is needed is a context-sensitive account of the evidence that does the job of eliminating possibilities.

4. CONTEXTUALISM, DEEP AND SUPERFICIAL

As I noted, Lewis's account of knowledge is a contextualist one, and most of his project in his paper, "Elusive Knowledge", is devoted to a detailed characterization of the contextual factors that are relevant to the interpretation of knowledge claims. Specifically, on Lewis's analysis, we are allowed to ignore certain unelimated possibilities, and the constructive project of his account of knowledge was to lay down a set of rules constraining the possibilities that are properly ignored. But the account of knowledge is basically a foundationalist one, and the contextualism is superficial: a way to reconcile common-sense talk about knowledge with a kind of Cartesian skepticism.

Let me use an analogy to try to explain what I have in mind in distinguishing a more superficial from a deeper kind of contextualism. There is a debate in the philosophical literature about whether it makes sense to quantify over absolutely everything. There is obviously no *set* of absolutely everything, or any other entity that constitutes the totality of everything, but some philosophers (Richard Cartwright, Tim Williamson, Agustin Rayo, e.g.) argue that the range of our quantifiers may consist of a plurality that is all-inclusive. Other philosophers (Charles Parsons, Michael Dummett, Michael Glanzberg, e.g.) have argued that there is no intelligible notion of absolutely everything: any domain can potentially be seen as partial, relative to something more inclusive. There is a complex mix of technical and philosophical issues here, and it is difficult to state the contrasting theses in a clear and neutral way. I don't want to enter into this debate in this context, but just to note that one issue on which it is clear that the philosophers on the opposite sides of this debate do not disagree about is this: quantifiers, as used in natural language as well as in many technical contexts are most often context-dependent quantifiers that range over contextually restricted domains. Both sides will agree that we may speak the literal truth when we say such things as that there is no beer left, that all the children are accounted for, that everyone has gone home. So both sides in this debate are contextualists about the quantifiers, but according to one, but not the other, the context-dependence is ineliminable, and so the contextualism is not just a fact about the way our language is used to generalize, but a fact about the nature of generality. For the absolutist, the contextualism about quantifiers is superficial: though we in fact often let implicit contextual factors restrict our domain, we need not do so. There is an absolute domain (if I may speak loosely, with a singular term to refer to what is properly spoken of only in the plural) of which all other domains are restrictions, and we could in principle make all of our contextual restrictions explicit.

The kind of context-dependence that Kaplan's original theory of indexicals and demonstratives was aiming to model is also superficial, in this sense. The context-dependence was in the relation between the expressions of the indexical language and the propositions that they expressed, but the propositions themselves ("content", or "what is said", as opposed to "character") were characterized independently of context. Later, when the phenomenon of essentially indexical attitudes was recognized, Kaplan's theory was applied to a deeper kind of context-dependence.

Lewis's contextualism about knowledge is superficial in exactly this sense. On his account, there is one privileged context for the interpretation of knowledge claims—the context in which none of the possibilities are properly ignored. This context has a privileged status, since all other contexts can be seen as restrictions on it. One might define an absolute concept of knowledge that built this privileged context into the analysis and expressed the restricted knowledge claims by putting the restriction into the content of the claim. (To know that *P* in a context in which certain possibilities are properly ignored is to know, absolutely, that *if* the ignored possibilities are unrealized, then *P*.) Such a concept of knowledge would differ semantically from Lewis's, but the epistemology would be essentially the same. It is tempting to think that what we *really* know, on the Lewis analysis, is what we know in the unrestricted context. The rest is just loose talk. (Remarks toward the end of Lewis's paper support the idea that he is inclined to succumb to this temptation. He suggests that ascriptions of knowledge are just a "handy but humble approximation," "one of the messy short-cuts . . . that we resort to because we are not smart enough to live up to really high, perfectly Bayesian standards of rationality."[10])

One might or might not be satisfied with this kind of response to skepticism, if it worked. But my problem with his analysis is not about the status of the rules that allow us to expand our knowledge beyond what is eliminated by experience, but rather about the assumption that phenomenal experience automatically brings knowledge. My complaint is not that he gratuitously permits possibilities to be ignored, but that he presumes an unjustifiably firm foundation for knowledge. Even in the skeptical context, Lewis's account implies that we know too much about

---

[10] Lewis (1996), 440.

the essential nature of our experience. We need a context, not to explain how we can go beyond our experience to eliminate possibilities, but to provide an account of the information that does the eliminating.

5. CONCEPTS: PHENOMENAL AND DEMONSTRATIVE

The story about Mary in the coin-flip scenario illustrates the complex relation between experience and evidence—that was its purpose. Just having the *experience* of seeing the red star was not enough to give Mary the *evidence* she needed to eliminate the alternative possibility that she was having an experience with a very different qualitative character (the qualitative character she would have had if she had seen a green star). But what *were* the epistemic consequences, for Mary, of leaving her room, and seeing color for the first time—what did she learn? It is tempting to say that what she did was to acquire a new *concept* for the qualitative property that she came to exemplify. She already had one concept of that property, before leaving her room, and after she was presented with the red star, she had two concepts, without knowing that they were concepts of the same property (just as Pierre had two concepts of London without knowing that they were concepts of the same city). The second concept Mary acquired, unlike the first, was a *pure phenomenal concept*, or perhaps a *demonstrative concept*. It is tempting to say this, and there may be something right about it, but I don't think these creatures of darkness—concepts—will help us to clarify what is going on. We can't avoid our problem by introducing an additional layer between the knower and the features of the world (or in this case, features of the subject) that are known. (The main attraction of concepts, I think, is that they facilitate equivocation between the vehicles of representation—the linguistic or mental objects or features that do the representing—and the meaning or content of the representation.)

So what are concepts? Some think of them as something like mental words—words of a language of thought. Presumably, their meanings are essential to them: to grasp a concept is to know its meaning. Or perhaps the concept *is* the meaning. But what is the meaning of the demonstrative or pure phenomenal concept that Mary acquired—the one that (following John Perry) she used the word "wow" to express? More specifically, is the concept that Mary acquired in the actual world (the world in which she was shown a red star) the same concept as the one she acquired in the alternative world in which she was presented with a green star? We know that Mary would have had a different kind of experience if she had been shown the green star, but would the *concept* that she acquired have been different? There are problems with each answer to this question.

If the two "wow" concepts are the same, then Mary knows what concept she is expressing, but that concept is only contingently connected to the experience itself, so it is not really a pure phenomenal concept, but a descriptive or perhaps demonstrative concept, identified by Mary's contextual situation, and her knowledge there, rather than by the intrinsic character of the experience. On the other hand, suppose the "wow" concepts expressed in the two possible worlds are different from each other. Suppose they are object-dependent concepts, identified by the phenomenal properties themselves—the qualia—to which they in fact refer. Then they might reasonably be called pure phenomenal concepts, but we will have to conclude that Mary does not know which of the two concepts it is that she is thinking. Her thought, on this account, will violate what Paul Boghossian calls, following Michael Dummett, a principle of *epistemic transparency*. (There are a number of different formulations of transparency principles of this kind that I will discuss, some more problematic than others, but what is violated here is a principle that requires Mary to know what concept she is deploying, where it is assumed that one knows what concept one is deploying if and only if one is deploying the same concept in all possible worlds that are epistemically possible at the time.[11]) On this horn of the dilemma, we have a direct connection between the content of Mary's thought and the qualitative character of the experience that the thought is about (a connection that perhaps constitutes her being *acquainted* with the character of the experience), but the cost is that we must say Mary is only indirectly connected to the content of her thought.

6. ACQUAINTANCE AND TRANSPARENCY

What is this mysterious epistemic relation that is supposed to connect us directly, either to our experience or to our thought about it, or to both? To be *acquainted* with an object, according to Russell, is to "have a direct cognitive relation to that object, i.e. [to be] directly aware of the object itself." The paradigm of objects of acquaintance, for Russell, were sensory experiences, but this same epistemic relation that connects us to our experience is supposed to connect us to the constituents of our thoughts: The thesis quoted at the head of this chapter, that *"every proposition which we can understand must be composed wholly of constituents with which we are acquainted"*, was for Russell a "fundamental principle". We may have moved beyond Russell's simple picture of the way we are related to the constituents of the contents of our thoughts, but the assumption that we stand in a distinctive and direct epistemic relation to the contents of thought persists. Michael Dummett, for

[11] Thanks to Scott Sturgeon for helping me to get clearer about the differences between different characterizations of transparency. He emphasized that this conception of phenomenal concepts does *not* violate a transparency principle that is formulated in terms of the subject's capacity to discriminate between two concepts within his conceptual repertoire. See Sturgeon (forthcoming).

example, asserts that "a thought is transparent in the sense that, if you grasp it, you thereby know everything to be known about it as it is in itself."[12] This sounds a lot like acquaintance. As we have seen, there are problems with the idea that we are acquainted with our sensory experience, problems that suggest that the paradigm cases of acquaintance may be a poor model for understanding our epistemic relation to the contents of our thoughts. But it can't be denied that there is some kind of special epistemic relation that we stand in to the contents of our thought—the problem is to pin down exactly what it is.

The identification of acquaintance with knowledge of essence that we saw in Lewis and others is also suggested by Dummett's statement about the transparency of thought. It echoes Lewis's principle of identification. The one says that we know the essence of our experience just by having it; the other says that we know everything essential to a thought simply by thinking it. In both cases, a thesis about our knowledge of experience, or propositional content, puts constraints on the nature of what is known: if the principles were correct, then experiences would have to be the kind of thing whose nature is fully revealed in the having of experience, and the contents of thought would have to be the kind of thing whose nature is fully revealed in the thinking of the thought. It is easy to see why, on this picture, the idea that a singular proposition could be the content of a thought must be rejected. The kind of internalist picture that accepted this principle of acquaintance will grant that individuals are involved in the characterization of the contents of thought (beliefs may, in a sense, be about London, or Bismarck), but will insist that thought is characterized only indirectly in terms of individuals. John McDowell gives an apt description of this internalist picture, which

---

[12] Dummett (1981), 51.

he attributes to Frege, and describes as "a suspect conception of how thought relates to reality":

When we mention an object in describing a thought we are giving only an extrinsic characterization of the thought (since the mention of the object takes us outside the subject's mind); but there must be an intrinsic characterization available (one which does not take us outside the subject's mind), and that characterization would have succeeded in specifying the essential core of the thought even if extra-mental reality had not obliged by containing the object.[13]

But of course properties and relations also have essential natures: knowing everything there is to be known about pineapples, or light bulbs, blueness, liquidity, fatherhood, inertia, as they are in themselves is at least as demanding as knowing the essential nature of London, or of Bismarck (or of the experience of seeing red). It is hard to see what resources there might be for specifying the essential core of any thought that do not take us outside of the subject's mind.

The alternative is to recognize that contents themselves are ways of characterizing a state of mind extrinsically. If a thought has, as its content, a singular proposition about London, it is because the ascriber of the thought can correctly characterize the world as the thinker takes it be as a function of London, which in the normal case can be done when possible worlds containing London are apt for describing that thinker's cognitive states. To describe a person's state of mind in terms of the objects, properties and relations that the attributor finds in the world is not to give an indirect or approximate characterization of an intentional state that might be described more directly. It is not that if we were to open up the person's mind and stare it in the face, we would find the content as it is in itself. There is, alas, only a brain in the head—no pieces of information, no contents,

13 McDowell (1977), 174–5.

wide or narrow. Propositions, whether they are Fregean thoughts, Russellian complexes, or sets of possible states of the world, are abstract objects that we use to represent certain capacities and dispositions of people, and certain kinds of social relations between them. There is, of course, a daunting general problem of saying what it is for a way the world might be (or a set of such ways) to represent the way the world is according to some person's beliefs or knowledge. The problems of intentionality and of knowledge are the problems of saying how believers and knowers must be related to the objects, properties and relations that are used to characterize the world according to them in order for the characterization to be correct. But what is required for a subject to have knowledge or belief about a particular individual (knowledge or belief with a singular proposition as its content) is not some very strong acquaintance relation with the individual, and it is also not some rich and detailed conception of it. These are neither necessary nor sufficient. As the familiar puzzle cases (the Babylonians and Hesperus/Phosphorus, Ralph and Ortcutt, Pierre and London/Londres, Mary and ph-red/wow, etc.) bring out, one may be strongly acquainted (in the ordinary sense of acquaintance) with some object, person or type of experience in different ways, and one may have different rich and detailed conceptions of an individual without realizing that they are different conceptions of the same individual. In such cases, one cannot (at least without some special contextual clues) aptly and unambiguously characterize the world as it is according to that person as a function of the individual. But in a normal case where one has, in context, a single dominant cognitive connection with an individual, one may unambiguously describe the world according to the thinker as a function of that individual, even if the connection is weak and one's conception of the object is thin and mostly inaccurate. Pierre, for example, knows much less about the city of Kiev than he knows about London, and perhaps what little he believes about this city is mistaken. But he has heard of it, and so we can correctly characterize the world according to Pierre by locating Kiev, the city itself, there, and we can correctly ascribe to Pierre belief in singular propositions about that city. We have to use *some* of the materials we find in the actual world to characterize the ways people take things to be (there is nothing else to use), and cities, people and physical objects are as good as anything else, in the right circumstances, for this purpose.[14]

But while I think it is an unavoidable fact about propositional content that it is the kind of thing that can be characterized only in terms of materials that are "external to the mind" of the subject whose thought has that content, there is a prima facie tension, much discussed in the philosophical literature, between this fact and the fact that it is the subject's perspective on the world that we are using content to characterize, and so the characterization can be correct only if the subject has, in some sense to be clarified, epistemic access to the contents of her own thought. In the next chapter, I will take a look at this tension, and argue that some of the apparatus we have been using may help to resolve it. While some are tempted to respond to the tensions by retreating to an internalist picture, I will suggest that an adequate response requires a move in the opposite direction, to a more thoroughgoing externalism.

[14] The preceding paragraph overlaps with some remarks toward the end of Stalnaker (2008).

6

Knowing What One is Thinking

It is an undeniable feature of the notion of meaning—obscure
as that notion is—that meaning is *transparent* in the sense
that, if someone attaches a meaning to each of two words,
he must know whether these meanings are the same.

Michael Dummett[1]

Paul Boghossian, in a discussion of the transparency of mental
content, quotes this formulation of a transparency thesis, which
is somewhat different from the formulation discussed in the last
chapter. This version of the thesis may avoid a commitment to a
conception of meaning or content as an internal object whose essential nature must be fully grasped, but it brings its own problems. The
principle is not, in any case, quite what we want, since our concern
(and Boghossian's concern in the context in which he quotes this
passage) is with the contents of thought, and not with the meanings
of words. The issue about thought is somewhat different from the
corresponding issue about linguistic expressions, and one source

---

[1] Dummett (1978), 131, quoted in Boghossian (1994), 33.

of unclarity in Dummett's thesis about meaning is unclarity about the relationship between the two issues. In the case of meaning, the issue concerns the relation between a representational vehicle, identified independently of its meaning, and a meaning that one "attaches" to it. The idea of attaching a meaning to a word is presumably to be explained in terms of the intentions with which the speaker uses the word—the intention to use the word with that meaning. If this is right, then understanding just what Dummett's transparency thesis says will require getting clear about the contents of the relevant intentions, and the speaker's epistemic relation to them: the issue about meaning will be parasitic on the issue about thought. The main point is not that issues about meaning in general are parasitic on issues about thought (although I think that they are). Dummett holds that the intentionality of thought should be explained in terms of the intentionality of speech, and if he is right about this, then the intentions to use words with certain meanings must ultimately be explained in terms of the speaker's capacities to use those words in a way that accords with the practices of his linguistic community. But however the contents of thoughts are explained, the transparency principle will presuppose that speakers and thinkers know the contents of the intentions that are involved in the attaching of meanings to words. One obviously cannot understand the "attaching" of contents to intentions and other thoughts in terms of the thinker's intentions that those thoughts should have the contents that they have.[2] I think that the assumption, implicit in much of the literature about the transparency of mental content, that the issue about thought closely parallels the issue about meaning tends to distort the former issue.

Boghossian divides the transparency thesis, modified to be about the contents of thought rather than the meanings of words, into

---

[2] Cf. the remarks on "purely voluntaristic view of reference" in the discussion of Lewis on Putnam's paradox in Ch. 1.

two parts, which he calls "transparency of sameness" and "transparency of difference":

(a) If two of a thinker's token thoughts possess the same content, then the thinker must be able to know *a priori* that they do; and (b) If two of a thinker's token thoughts possess distinct contents, then the thinker must be able to know *a priori* that they do.[3]

He defends these principles, arguing that they are a necessary part of any adequate account of intentionality:

We don't just ascribe thoughts to a person in order to say something descriptively true of him. We use such ascriptions for two related purposes: on the one hand, to enable assessments of his rationality and, on the other to explain his behavior. As these matters are currently conceived, a thought must be epistemically transparent if it is to play these roles.[4]

He also argues that the principles of epistemic transparency cannot be reconciled with the anti-individualist[5] account of the facts that give thoughts their content that Tyler Burge and others have defended, and that is implicit in the kind of picture that I have been promoting.

I agree with Boghossian that we ascribe thought in order to explain action, and to assess the reasoning of thinkers, and that such explanations and assessments cannot turn on facts that are inaccessible to the subject. If we could be wrong, on empirical grounds, about the contents of our own thoughts, then we could be wrong, on empirical grounds, about the validity of our reasoning, and this seems incompatible with the idea that we can separate the assessment of reasoning from assessment of the truth

---

[3] Boghossian (1994), 36.   [4] Ibid., 39.

[5] I use the term "anti-individualism"—introduced, in the relevant sense, by Tyler Burge—for the thesis that the property of having a thought with a certain intentional content is a relational rather than an intrinsic property of the thinker. The thesis is often labeled "externalism", but I don't want to confuse this specific thesis with the more general externalist approach to intentionality. There are connections: I think the anti-individualist thesis is motivated by the general approach, but one could accept an externalist formulation of the problem of intentionality, while arguing for individualism about mental content.

of the premises on which the reasoning is based. As Lewis and Kripke agreed, if a theory is forced to say that Pierre, because of his factual mistake, has contradictory beliefs, there is something wrong with the theory. But I think an anti-individualist account of the facts that determine content can be reconciled with a suitably qualified version of a principle of epistemic transparency. I won't defend the principles of the transparency of sameness and difference exactly as Boghossian states them, nor will I provide an alternative formulation. My aim is just to show that an anti-individualist thesis about content attribution is compatible with an account of reasoning that is clear about the difference between errors of reasoning and errors of fact, as Boghossian rightly says that any adequate account must be. As with the puzzles about Lewis's account of the role of experience in eliminating possibilities, I will suggest that the puzzles about knowledge of content involve a mixing of internal and external perspectives, and that if we give a thoroughly externalist account both of knowledge and of the role of content in the characterization of states of mind, we can give a plausible account of what we know and what we do not know about what we are thinking.

1. SLOW SWITCHING

The argument of Boghossian's that I will focus on uses a twin-earth thought experiment to try to show a conflict between the transparency of difference and anti-individualism. I will use his example, since it is his argument that I want to discuss, though I think the example involves an unnecessary amount of science fiction. The same point could be made with a more down-to-earth case, about which intuitions might be clearer, and I will later describe some more homey examples that have a similar structure. But first, I will tell his story, which derives from an example of Tyler Burge's, sketch Boghossian's argument, and then say how the story should be modeled in the framework that we have been using, and how the argument might be answered in the context of this model. After sketching a number of less exotic examples that I think help to bring out different aspects of the underlying problem, I will conclude by saying what I think the moral of the story is.

Twin Earth, in this story, is not a counterfactual world, but a part of the actual world (as it was in Hilary Putnam's original thought experiment). The story concerns an unfortunate earthling, Peter, who "is suddenly and unwittingly transported to Twin Earth," where he "suffers no discernible disruption in the continuity of his mental life," but "happily lives out the rest of his days, never discovering the relocation that he has been forced to undergo."[6] Now it is clear (at least on the usual assumptions about the moral of the original Twin Earth thought experiments) that the thoughts expressed with the word 'water' that Peter thinks when he first arrives on Twin Earth are thoughts about water, and not about twin-water, the Twin Earth substitute (with chemical composition XYZ). When (immediately after the unwitting switch) Peter looks out on a lake, which is actually filled with XYZ rather than H_2O, he forms the false belief that there is water in the lake. But after a certain amount of time goes by, all parties agree, it seems intuitively right to say that the thoughts Peter would express with the same word 'water' would come to be thoughts about twin-water. At the later time, when he looks out at the same lake and thinks a thought that he would express the same way, his thought is one that is true if and only if there is XYZ in the lake.

This kind of thought experiment has come to be called a "slow switching" scenario. There are two switches: first Peter is switched from one environment to another, and the intuition is that a second switch, this time in the content of his thoughts, will follow some time later. Let me sketch a simple model of

---

[6] Boghossian (1994), 37.

the story, using the kind of representation of a state of belief in terms of possible worlds that I have been using. I say "simple", but the story is complicated, as well as oversimplified. It will at least illustrate the general method that I think helps to clarify the content of someone's thought in problematic cases. One begins by asking, what the world is like according to that person, using our resources to describe the world as that person takes it to be.

I will consider just three representative possible worlds, and what is going on at three different times in each of these worlds. First there is the actual world, **a**, in which the surreptitious switch took place. Second, there is a world, **w**, in which no switch ever took place, and in which the life Peter led on earth was (after the time of the actual switch) just like the life he actually led on Twin Earth. Finally, there is a possible world, **x**, in which no switch took place, but in which Peter was born and raised on Twin Earth, rather than on Earth, and in which he also lived a life that was (from the inside) just like the life he led in the other two possible worlds. The three times in question are a time, t_0, before the actual transportation, a time t_1, very soon after the actual transportation (but before the alleged semantic switch), and a time t_2, much later, when, according to Boghossian's story, Peter's thoughts expressed with the world "water" are thoughts about Twin-water, or XYZ. In each of these worlds, and at each time, there is a lake that he is looking at, and thinking a somewhat pedestrian thought that he would express (at each time and in each world) by saying "there is water in that lake."

We might add a family of contrasting worlds that includes some that Peter is distinguishing from one or another of the possible worlds I have described. These are worlds just like **a**, **w**, and **x**, except that the relevant lake is dry. (Imagine that this lake is like the reservoir on the Stanford campus that is dry during some parts of year and full at other times.) The idea is that when Peter thinks, at each time and in each world, a thought that he would express with the sentence "there is water in the lake", he is distinguishing it, in his thought, from a situation in which the lake is then dry.

Now we can ask a series of questions about Peter's knowledge and beliefs: First, which of these possible worlds are compatible with Peter's beliefs, and with his knowledge, at each time? Second, what is the content of the thought that Peter thinks, in each of the possible worlds, and at each of the times? Since we will be considering a problem for the anti-individualist about content, we will be asking what the externalist, or anti-individualist, should say about each of these questions.

The answers to all the questions (given the anti-individualist assumptions) are clear: in the actual world, a, Peter's thoughts at t_0 and t_1 are about water, and his thought at t_2 is about twater. In counterfactual world w, his thought is about water at all three times, and in counterfactual world x his thought is about twater at all three times. Peter's epistemic alternatives, at times t_0 and t_1 in world a, are a and w; his epistemic alternatives at the same two times in w are also a and w, and his epistemic alternatives at t_2 (after the semantic shift) in the actual world, and in world x are a and x. It is straightforward to see that at each time, and in each world, the content of Peter's thought is the same at the relevant time in each of the possible worlds that is compatible with what he knows at that time. He knows, in all cases, what the contents of his thoughts are at the time. The model gives an explicit implementation of the externalist's general strategy for reconciling his theory with knowledge of content, a strategy summed up succinctly by Davidson, and quoted by Boghossian: "Showing that there is no conflict [between externalism and knowledge of content] is basically simple. It depends on realizing that whatever is responsible for the contents of our thoughts, whether known or not, is also responsible for the content of the thought that we have the thought."[7]

---

[7] Boghossian (1994), 35, quoting an unpublished Davidson paper.

This seems to dissolve the problem, so long as we are focusing on Peter's cognitive situation at each of the separate times, but as Boghossian emphasizes, the externalist's strategy is more problematic when we consider Peter's thoughts, at one time, about his thoughts at another time. Peter might, at time t_2, remember a thought that he had at one of the earlier times, and put it together with a current thought. Suppose, for example, that at t_2, Peter thinks, "I remember thinking, back at t_0, that there was water in the lake I was then looking at." He then reasons, in his usual pedestrian fashion, "there was water in that lake, there is water in this lake, so there was water in both lakes," Boghossian argues that the externalist is committed to saying that in this case, we have a violation of the transparency principle. Peter is making a *logical*, and not a *factual* mistake in this reasoning—a fallacy of equivocation—since the two "water" thoughts involve distinct concepts that Peter treats, in his thought, as the same.

Boghossian's argument assumes that the content of the thought that Peter had at the earlier time must be the same as the content of his later thought when he is recalling the earlier thought. One strategy for responding to the argument is to reject this assumption.[8] There is no question that Peter *thinks* that the earlier thought had the same content that the corresponding current thought has, but he might be mistaken about this without violating transparency. No one thinks that we have special access to what we were thinking at an earlier time. According to this response, the earlier thought about what was in that lake was about H_2O, while the later thought about the earlier event was a thought about XYZ. Peter is making a straightforward factual mistake when he says or thinks (at the later time) a thought that he would then express this way: "At the earlier time, when I said to myself 'There is water in this lake', I was thinking that there was water in that

---

[8] Tye (1988) uses this strategy to defend the compatibility of externalism with transparency.

lake." His reasoning is logically fine—it is just that one of the premises is false. But, Boghossian replies, "surely memory failure is not the point." It is, he says, a platitude that "if S knows that p at t_0, and if at (some later time) t_2, S remembers everything S knew at t_0, then S knows that p at t_2."[9] Boghossian is surely right that it would misdescribe the situation to say that Peter's memory failed, or he *forgot* what he was thinking at the earlier time. What he calls a platitude certainly sounds like one, although there are different ways to understand what it says: we might accept the platitude without agreeing that Peter either *forgot* what he knew at the earlier time, or else he still remembers it. There may be other ways for knowledge to change over time than by learning and forgetting, and I will consider an example later where this is clearly what one should say.

Some who want to reconcile anti-individualism with transparency will concede Boghossian's point about memory, and question the argument at a different point. Tyler Burge, in his response to this problem, emphasizes the importance of what he calls "preservative memory":

If S has forgotten nothing, I see no reason to think that S will not know (in the relevant sense) at time t_2 what he knew at t_1.... S can at t_2 remember his thinking at t_1, and his memory can link the content of his earlier thought to that of the memory induced one. Merely by being in the second environment, with concepts appropriate to that environment, does not prevent him from retaining and thinking thoughts appropriate to the first.[10]

According to Burge's strategy for responding to Boghossian's argument, there is no equivocation because even though the reasoning occurs at the later time, both premises are unequivocally about *water* rather than *twater*. The second thought involved in the reasoning picks up its reference from the first. Burge suggests that Boghossian's argument "overlooks the centrality of preservative

---

[9] Boghossian (1989), 23.   [10] Burge (1998), 357.

memory in reasoning, and fails to note the particular character of the relation between the different concepts within the individual's cognitive system."[11] The view seems to be this: In the original story, when no thought taken from memory was involved, Peter's thought at t_2 was about twater. But in a context in which the memory thought is in play at that time, the thought Peter would express the same way will have a different content: it will be about water.

Some have found Burge's strategy implausible, since it requires saying that the concepts deployed, and the propositions thought and expressed, at a single time may depend on the surrounding situation, perhaps even on the order in which a sequence of thoughts takes place. Suppose Peter were *first* to think (at t_2) "there is water in this lake," as in the original story, and only then to remember his earlier thought. Does the remembered thought then pick up its reference from the current one, or does the content of the current thought shift when the earlier thought is remembered?[12]

Each of these responses to Boghossian's argument may appear strained, but I think the source of this appearance is that there is something misleading about locating the cognitive "shift" in Peter, rather than in the context in which knowledge is attributed to him, or in the circumstances that are appropriate for describing his cognitive situation. In the original story, what happens is that at the later, but not the earlier time, Peter's capacities and dispositions are most naturally described as a function of the substance XYZ, rather than the substance H_2O. If knowledge is, in a sense, lost and gained, or if the content ascribed to a token thought depend on the surrounding circumstances, it is because the space of possibilities that is relevant to the theorist's characterization of the subject's

<hr/>

[11] Burge (1998), 366.

[12] Jessica Brown argued that "the combination of views that Burge holds—that a slow switch subject may unwittingly have two distinct concepts that she expresses by a single term, but that cannot both figure in a single piece of reasoning—is counterintuitive and poorly motivated." See Brown (2004), 177 ff.

cognitive capacities changes, or depends on those circumstances. The anti-individualist must concede that it is difficult to describe, in a straightforward way, the changes in Peter's cognitive situation; his massive error about relevant changes in his environment involves a mismatch between changes in his environment and changes in the way he represents them. But we can give a coherent description of his cognitive situation that is compatible with a reasonable version of Boghossian's transparency principle.

The debate about how to understand the slow switching scenario is often framed as the question whether our unfortunate character has (at the later time) one "water" concept or two. Does Peter lose one concept, and gain another, at the time of the "switch", or does he keep the old concept when he gains the new one, while systematically confusing them with each other? This way of putting the problem suggests that the issue is about Peter's internal cognitive mechanism: does he have two different file folders labeled "water" in his mental file cabinet, one old and one new, or did he throw out the old one, moving its contents into the new one, when the switch occurred? But the arguments about the issue do not consider evidence about the form that mental representation takes, an issue on which we can only speculate, and the forms of representation do not seem to be relevant. This is another place where I think talk of concepts is not helpful. If what we mean by a concept is something like a mental word, and if it is assumed that Peter's thoughts about what he calls "water" are realized in the tokening of mental words, then it would seem most plausible to assume that Peter has just one word, whose meaning and extension shifts because of changes in his relation to his environment. Perhaps the meaning is essential to the identity of the concept, so that this counts as a substantial change, or perhaps it is not, so that it counts as an alteration of the concept. Either way, to take this model seriously requires strong theoretical assumptions about the form in which thoughts are represented. Specifically, it requires a commitment to the possibility of identifying a particular kind of representational vehicle independently of its intentional properties. Our model of Peter's evolving cognitive situation makes no assumptions about the form that his mental representations take.

2. VARIATIONS ON THE STORY

There are less exotic examples of the phenomenon that is illustrated by the story of Peter's unfortunate travels. I will look at four more stories, first since I think that more realistic stories are more reliable sources of intuitive judgment, and second because the range of cases help to bring out different aspects of the problem.

(i) Consider the case of Harvey, who revisits, years later, an island where he had spent a memorable childhood vacation. Or so he believes. But in fact the island he visits as an adult is a different one. "Treasure Island" was Harvey's childhood private name for the place. "Treasure Island is not unspoiled, charming and exciting the way it used to be," Harvey muses on what he believes is his visit back to the place. He reaches this comparative judgment by putting his memory of the original island together with his current observation of the different one. No logical error here. His belief, at the time, that he would express by saying "I am now on Treasure Island" is simply factually false.

Despite his disappointment, Harvey keeps going back, year after year, and comes to know the place very well. Many years later, he thinks to himself as he reads the weather report before leaving for his annual vacation, "I see that it is going to be a rainy week on Treasure Island." (Of course the report he was reading did not use the name "Treasure Island", since that is Harvey's private name, but that is how he would have expressed the thought that he had on reading the report.) It seems right to say that the first thought was about the original Treasure Island, but that the later thought is about the new island, which has in the meantime become the dominant source of Harvey's beliefs that he would express with this name. On the other hand, if he were to put his current belief about the weather on "Treasure Island" together with something he remembers ("It seems to be a lot rainier now on Treasure Island than it was in my youth"), it is less clear which of the two islands we should take his thought to be about. Throughout the story, there is only one relevant island in the world as Harvey takes it to be, and there is no question of memory failure from earlier to later time. The problem is that there are *two* relevant islands in the actual world, and we need to say which of them is the one island in the world as it is according to Harvey. The shift from one answer to the other is not a result of a change in Harvey's internal cognitive apparatus. It reflects a difference in the circumstances that make one rather than the other of these islands the more appropriate candidate to use to describe his state of mind.

(ii) Keith Donnellan told a story, a long time ago in the course of defending a causal theory of reference, that has a very similar structure. A man is introduced at a party to a student, who he is told is the famous philosopher, J. L. Aston-Martin. In fact, it is a different person (perhaps with the same name). When the student reports, after the party, that he met J. L. Aston-Martin last night, he refers to the famous philosopher, and what he says is false. But (Donnellan argues) when he is narrating certain events that took place at the party (" . . . and then Robinson tripped over Aston-Martin's feet and fell flat on his face"), he is referring to the man he was introduced to, and speaks the truth.[13]

Donnellan put the emphasis, not on a temporal change, as information that has the new person as its causal source grows and becomes dominant, but rather on the purposes to which the information or misinformation is being put, and on the context of attribution. He does mention, in a footnote, a version of the story

[13] Donnellan (1972), 370 ff.

that anticipates the slow switching scenario (he supposes that the person met at the party becomes a longer term acquaintance of the student, without the mistaken belief ever being corrected), but he says that even at the later time, if the student made a remark, using the name "Aston-Martin" whose point depended on the referent being the famous philosopher, then we would take his statement, and the corresponding thought, to be about him. If the relevant contrast is instead between possible situations involving the whereabouts of a recent acquaintance, then one should take what is said, or thought, to be about the person the student met at the party. There need be no stable temporal switch in the student's cognitive state, so if we were to force the issue into the "one concept or two" mold, we will have to say that the student has both concepts at once (perhaps realized in the same mental name), and beliefs at one time both about the famous philosopher, and the man he met at the party. But one should still not represent his reasoning as involving unwitting equivocation. In any one context, we should take his beliefs to be about one of the men, or about the other. Suppose, for example, he reasons, "I see that Aston-Martin is scheduled to give a talk in Oxford today, but I just saw him in the bookstore, so he must have canceled it." Even though the source of one piece of information is one of the two "Aston-Martin"s and the source of the second piece of information is the other, we still will take his reasoning to involve a factually false premise, rather than a fallacy of equivocation. The reason we do this is that, as Boghossian emphasizes in motivating the transparency principle, we attribute content in order to assess reasoning, and to explain behavior.

Each of the three stories I have discussed so far involves a change over time in the situation of the subject, a shift in the dominant causal source of the beliefs that he would express with a certain word or name, but this was only one of the considerations in the choice of a context to represent the cognitive situation of the subject at the different times. The contrasts that are relevant to the explanation of the actions, reactions and reasoning of the subject also play a role. And there are cases that are similar to these stories in that the subject falsely identifies distinct things, and so threaten a violation of the transparency of difference, but which involve no temporal shift at all.[14]

(iii) Consider this reversal of the situation in John Perry's example of the ship *Enterprise*:[15] This time, there are in fact two different ships seen in the Oakland harbor that are taken to be the same ship. Behind the large building, the bow of the *Enterprise* is visible on the left, as in the original example, but behind the building on the right, it is the stern of a different shorter ship that is blocking the view of the stern of the *Enterprise*. John believes that *this* ship (looking at the bow of the *Enterprise*) is the same as *that* one (looking at the stern of the second ship). Now suppose John were to reason as follows: This ship is an aircraft carrier (based on observing the bow of the ship on the right); this ship is British (observing the British flag flying from the stern of the second ship); therefore, there is a British aircraft carrier in the harbor.[16] Does this reasoning involve a logical error? If we look first at a linguistic expression of the argument, we might contrast two cases:

(A)   (P1) *This* ship (pointing to the bow) is an aircraft carrier;
      (P2) *This* ship (pointing to the stern of the second ship) is British;
      Therefore, . . .

(B)   (P1) *This* ship (pointing to the bow) is an aircraft carrier.
      (P2) *It* (observing the flag on the stern of the second ship) is British;
      Therefore, ...

[14] John Hawthorne made this point in discussion after the lecture on which this chapter is based, using the same kind of example that I will give.

[15] See Ch. 4 for a discussion of the original case.

[16] The inference, of course, involves a background presupposition that the relevant ship or ships demonstrated are in the harbor.

In case (B), it is clear that, although the *evidence* on which (P2) is based comes from the second ship, the *claim* made in that statement is about the first ship, since the pronoun is anaphoric. So there is no equivocation; the argument is straightforwardly valid, although the second premise, and the conclusion are false. If the reasoning had begun with the premise based on the observation of the British ship, then both premises would have been about *that* ship. The analysis of this case will straightforwardly parallel Burge's analysis of the case of Peter when he puts a remembered thought together with a current one.[17] (And it will not seem problematic, in this case, that the content of the premises depends on their order.) But what about argument (A)? Here it seems clear that the two premises are about different ships, and so both are true. But the conclusion is false, so isn't John making an unwitting logical error? Isn't he mistakenly confusing the proposition that *this* ship is an aircraft carrier with the distinct proposition that *that* one is? Here I think the best way for the theorist to represent the reasoning is to take it to involve a false tacit presupposition, a suppressed premise, that *this* ship is *that* one, rather than a false belief that the two thoughts have the same content.[18] This way of representing the reasoning does not assume that John has entertained the possibility that the two ships are different—the possibility that distinguishes the two propositions—or that the presupposition that excludes this possibility is in any way encoded at some perhaps subpersonal level in John's internal cognitive apparatus. Most of what we presuppose is presupposed simply by not recognizing the possibilities in which the presuppositions are false. The explicit statement of the tacit premise is part of the theorist's representation of the situation.

[17] In defending his analysis, Burge pointed to an analogy between preservative memory and anaphoric reference.

[18] According to a Kaplanian semantics for demonstratives, the two demonstratives are rigid designators, so that the statement or thought, "*this* ship is the same as *that* one" is necessarily false. What is presupposed is not the necessarily false proposition, but the contingent one that John would have been expressing if he said, in this situation, "*this* ship is the same as *that* one."

If the skeptical visitor, who in Perry's original example of the *Enterprise* refused to believe that *this* ship was the same as *that* one, were present in this version of the story (this time vindicated by the facts), then the possibility that distinguishes the two propositions will be explicitly recognized. And even in a situation in which John never considered the possibility that there was more than one ship visible in the harbor, he would still have no difficulty understanding a claim that *this* ship is an aircraft carrier, while *that* one is not, and would not take the claim to be a simple contradiction. So I think it is reasonable to say that, while John has the correct belief that the two statements (that *this* is an aircraft carrier and that *that* is one) distinguish between the possibilities compatible with what he is presupposing in the same way, we need not say that he believes that they express the same proposition, relative to a wider range of possibilities.

We have contrasted two linguistic formulations of a piece of reasoning, but our concern is with *mental* content. Suppose John did not put his reasoning into words: he just glanced back and forth between the two ships, and silently drew the conclusion from his observations. Suppose that the possibility that there were *two* ships visible in the harbor never even crossed his mind. Which of the contrasting patterns, (A) or (B), best fits this case? Was his reasoning uniformly about one of the ships, or about the other, or was it about both, with a false suppressed premise to connect the two observations? These different ways of representing John's reasoning differ with respect to the truth values of the contents of his thoughts only relative to possible worlds that were not on his horizon; his thoughts were focused on contrasts between certain possible situations, and the different representations of his reasoning agree on the identity of the relevant propositions, relative to those possible situations. The case is a puzzle case because the *actual* world, which is always a relevant possibility, is not among those that the subject took himself to be distinguishing between, and the different representations of the reasoning say different things about the truth values of the premises, relative to the actual world. The facts about John's cognitive situation may not settle the question of which representation is correct.

(iv) Let me look briefly at one more example, one that connects with the issues about self-locating knowledge and belief: Alice tells Bert, at the Saturday night party (at about 11 p.m.), that tomorrow is her birthday. Later that evening (at about 12:15 a.m.) Clara tells Bert that tomorrow is *her* birthday. Bert (mistakenly assuming that it is not yet midnight), thinks, "what a coincidence: Alice and Clara have the same birthday." Bert retained the belief he acquired from Alice, and put this information together with his new information about Clara, and made an inference from them. Both Alice and Clara spoke the truth, but the conclusion Bert drew from their statements was false. Did he make a logical error?

In this case, a response analogous to the first response that we considered in the case of Peter seems to be appropriate. Recall the dialectic of that response: The suggestion was that Peter is just factually mistaken when he thinks, "At the earlier time, when I said to myself 'There is water in this lake', I was thinking that there was water in that lake." The claim was that this is not a violation of transparency, since transparency does not assume that we have special access to the contents of our earlier thoughts. Boghossian's response was that "surely memory failure is not the point," and I agreed that it would obviously be wrong to say that Peter *forgot* what he was thinking then. But, it was suggested, perhaps knowledge can be lost in other ways than by forgetting. Whether or not this strategy of response is plausible in the case of Peter, it does seem right to say the following in this case, strange as it may sound: Bert is mistaken when he thinks (at the later time), "When I said to myself, a little while ago, 'Alice's birthday is tomorrow', I was then thinking that Alice's birthday is tomorrow." Boghossian's platitude about memory ("if S knows that p at t_1, and if at (some later time) t_2, S remembers everything S knew at t_1, then

S knows that p at t_2") looks less platitudinous when it is applied to essentially self-locating knowledge.

In the context of our model of self-locating knowledge and belief, it is clear enough what is going on in this example: Bert is falsely presupposing that the two token thoughts took place on the same day, and relative to the possible worlds compatible with that presupposition, the two thoughts do have the same content. (That is, the functions from possible worlds to truth values, restricted to the domain of possible worlds compatible with that presupposition, are identical.) The reasoning that takes place against the background of that presupposition is correct reasoning; the problem is that the presupposition is factually false.

3. THE MORAL OF THE STORY

The most prominent examples of identity confusion in the philosophical literature about propositional attitudes are cases where one thing appears, to the thinker, in two different guises: The Babylonians and Hesperus/Phosphorus, Ralph and Ortcutt on the beach, and in the bar, Pierre and London/Londres, John and the *Enterprise*, bow and stern, Mary and wow/ph-red. Equally interesting are the cases of two things in the actual world merged into one in the world according to the thinker. The slow switching case, and the four variants that I have described, are just examples of this kind.

As I understand it, Boghossian's view of the target of his criticism is an essentially internalist picture, with an externalist component grafted onto it. Our thoughts are something like internal sentences to which we have access because they are part of the internal mental world. But (this is the externalist part) these mental sentences, individuated by their content, have essential properties that are extrinsic to the mind, and so are not accessible to the person who is thinking the thought. But we shouldn't think of access to our thought as access to an internal vehicle of representation. According to a more thoroughly externalist picture, we should think of the representation of states of knowledge and belief, and the content of occurrent thoughts, this way: Thinkers are things with a capacity to make their actions depend on the way the world is, and with dispositions to make their actions depend on the way they take the world to be. Theorists and attributors of thought characterize these capacities and dispositions by locating the world as the thinker takes it to be in a space of relevant alternative possibilities. The theorist uses actual things and properties to describe these possibilities, and that is why content depends on facts about the actual world. These things that attributors use to describe the possibilities will always be things that have essential natures—everything does—and it may be that both the attributor and the thinker being described are ignorant of these essential features. When the way the world actually is diverges from the way the subject takes it to be with respect to the identity and nature of things, and in particular when he or she conflates distinct things, or thinks of one thing as two, or when the changes in the world as it is diverge from changes in the world as it is taken to be, we may find it difficult to characterize a world according to the thinker that is apt for describing that person's cognitive capacities and dispositions. But our descriptive resources are rich and flexible, and in context, we can usually find a way. What counts as a correct description of the world according to the thinker may depend on the attributor's context. A principle of epistemic transparency is satisfied, according to this picture, not because the thinker is directly acquainted with an inner object that has an inner content essentially, but because an apt description of a thinker's cognitive state, if it is to explain the rational capacities and dispositions it is intended to explain, must represent the way the world is according to the thinker in a way that satisfies it.

7

After the Fall

Adam's one task in the Garden had been to invent language, to give each creature and thing its name. In that state of innocence, his tongue had gone straight to the quick of the world. His words had not been merely appended to the things he saw, they had revealed their essences, had literally brought them to life. A thing and its name were interchangeable. After the fall, this was no longer true. Names became detached from things, words devolved into a collection of arbitrary signs; language had been severed from God. The story of the Garden, therefore, records not only the fall of man, but the fall of language.

Paul Auster[1]

I have been promoting, throughout this book, a certain general picture—an externalist perspective on a subject's point of view. I have also been promoting some apparatus that I find useful for articulating the picture, and for clarifying some of the problems that it raises. The apparatus aims to provide a way to represent an objective conception of the world as it is in itself—an absolute conception, as Bernard Williams called it—and also to provide resources for clarifying the relation between such a conception and the perspectives of subjects who are part of the world (according

---

[1] Auster (1985), 52.

to our objective conception), and who have the capacity to experience and think about it. I think the apparatus helps to sharpen the issues, but it must be acknowledged that it also reveals some tensions in the picture that are not fully resolved. I am going to conclude with some impressionistic remarks that take us back to the general issues that I discussed at the beginning.

The critics of the internalist picture that I caricatured in Chapter 1 like to talk about it in mythic terms. Wilfrid Sellars's phrase, "the myth of the given" had resonance, even if it was not entirely clear exactly what the myth was. The quotation that heads this chapter uses an authentic myth that I think highlights one aspect of this picture. The words are those of a somewhat unhinged fictional scholar, interpreting Milton's *Paradise Lost*, but David Chalmers, quite independently, uses the same myth in a similar way, and connects it more explicitly with philosophical issues about perception and representation:

In the Garden of Eden, we had unmediated contact with the world. We were directly acquainted with objects in the world and with their properties. Objects were presented to us without causal mediation and properties were revealed to us in their true intrinsic glory.

When an apple in Eden looked red to us, the apple was gloriously, perfectly, and primitively *red*. . . . The qualitative redness in our experience derived entirely from the presentation of perfect redness in the world.

Eden was a world of perfect color. But then there was a Fall.[2]

The philosophers I have been criticizing know that we are no longer in the garden, but they would like at least to hold onto the idea that we can locate a kind of intentional foundation—a place where our thought attaches directly to its subject matter. In the garden (according to this way of interpreting the myth), we were directly connected to things in the outside world, but after our expulsion from Eden, we were connected in this way only to the materials within our separate internal worlds, to the

---

[2] Chalmers (2006).

qualitative character of our experience, and to the contents of the thought that we spin out of these materials. On this picture, the idea of separation and alienation from the world that comes with the myth of the garden seems apt. My aim in this book has been to undermine the foundationalist picture by undermining the idea that we have the kind of direct connection that the picture requires even to the contents of our minds. The point, of course, is not that we are even more alienated from the world than the internalist thinks; it is that we need a different way of thinking about what it is that connects our thought with its subject matter, a view of ourselves, not as separated from the external world, but as embedded in it, and interacting with it. That is our starting point. As I noted in Chapter 1, this kind of externalist shift, with its rejection of the foundationalist starting point, is a familiar theme that has taken various forms, and that shaped many of the philosophical debates of the twentieth century. It is a continuing theme: Tim Williamson's attacks on a principle of luminosity, for example, and his defense of what he calls cognitive homelessness use a different battery of arguments to develop and defend the same kind of picture that has been guiding me in developing the arguments in this book.[3] Perhaps the cognitive home we don't have (and if the truth be told, never had) is the Garden of Eden.

But the externalist shift, and the rejection of a foundation, brings its own set of problems, and perhaps the shift in view is naturally seen (as the myth suggests) as a loss of innocence. On a more sober account of the foundationalist picture that sets aside the colorful rhetoric about words revealing the essences of things, what is promised is a way to factor our theorizing about the world into two parts: first, we form, a priori, a conception of the logical space of possibilities (stipulating what we shall mean by the words we use to describe the possibilities). Then we gather evidence to discover where in that space of possibilities the actual world is

---

[3] Williamson (2001).

located. If we could theorize in this way, then we would have a general platform on which any disputes about the facts, or about deductive relationships, could be clarified and settled by methods that were neutral between any issues that might be contested. The central problem with this picture is that the meanings of our terms and the contents of our thoughts are determined by facts about our causal relations with things in the world, and with their properties and the relations between them, and so there is no general way, guaranteed to be neutral, to describe the space of possibilities in which we are trying to locate the world, or to characterize the evidence that would do the work of locating it in that space. We need, in order to sharpen and settle any particular dispute, a context in which we can separate (relative to that context) substantive from semantic issues: issues about how we characterize a space of relevant possibilities from issues about where in that space the actual world is located. But there is no general procedure for finding such a context; the task of doing so needs to be carried out on a case by case basis, and there is no guarantee that it will succeed. This essential contextualist feature of the account of rational debate and inquiry gives rise to a general worry that the externalist shift may involve a retreat from a robust realism. The externalist—the philosopher who begins in the middle—rejects a demand that his metaphysical commitments be justified from within, but he must accept the demand that his overall philosophical conception be in harmony with the possibility that the subjects in the world as he takes it to be (which include himself) should be the kind of thing that can have a conception of the kind that he has. This demand for harmony requires that we recognize that the theorist who is defending this general contextualist account of knowledge and representation is himself characterizing the world by distinguishing between relevant alternatives in a particular (philosophical) context. I think the essentially contextual account of knowledge, and of our intentional relations to the things we think about can be reconciled with a realist interpretation of knowledge and thought, but it takes philosophical work to do so.

The central feature of the apparatus in which I have developed the externalist and anti-foundationalist picture is the representation of intentional content in terms of the possible states of the world that provide the truth conditions for what we think and say. The most sharply focused critical arguments that I have given are directed at a cluster of theses defended by David Lewis, who shares with me a commitment to the possible worlds framework, though he interprets and applies it in a different way. It is the common ground that I share with Lewis that makes it possible for the criticisms to be as focused as they are, and some who accept the force of those arguments may conclude that the real source of the problems with the cluster of theses that Lewis defends is in his commitment to this framework. My view is that the clarity and explicitness in the representation of intentional content in terms of possible worlds brings out problems that are there for all of us. Every framework has its presuppositions and limitations, but if one is willing to talk of propositions at all, it is hard to avoid the idea that they *have* truth conditions, and that their truth conditions are essential to them. If this is right then this notion of content, even if it is only a partial account, does capture a feature of intentionality that everyone should recognize.

The main aim of the machinery for characterizing representational states that I have been promoting (the possible worlds framework, the account of self-locating belief, and of the representation of context) is to clarify the metaphysical issues by being as explicit as we can about the relation between a conception of the world as it is in itself and the features of a representation that essentially involve the subject's perspective on the world, and by providing resources for connecting the contents of what is said, thought or known in one context, with what is said, thought or known in another. One reason it is useful to think of propositions as functions from a given domain of possible worlds to truth values is that it allows one to make sense of the idea that the content of what is said or thought may be defined relative to narrower or wider domains of possibilities. So a proposition, understood this way, may be a piece of contextually local information, or it may be a piece of information that can be detached from the local context and applied more widely. And we can see propositions of the latter kind as extensions of propositions of the former kind. The framework aims to give resources for explaining how we calibrate the information expressed or thought in different contexts by a subject over time, or by different subjects in different situations. We begin, it is natural to think, in more local contexts, talking and thinking about ourselves and our immediate perceptual environment. We then develop means for expanding our representational resources, and for incorporating information from different contexts into more inclusive contexts. Doing this will involve representing ourselves and our local contexts within a more robust and inclusive context, and representing, in our conception of the world as it is in itself, the relations between ourselves and the things we represent (what John Perry called reflexive content). In the end, we must recognize that even our most stable and robust representations have the content that they have in virtue of our relations to what we represent. For example, we distinguished, in our account of self-locating belief, between a local representation of a time as *now* or *today* from an objective representation as 10 a.m., or Tuesday in order to represent cases where a person doesn't know what time or day it is. But our objective labels for times got their reference from events and processes that stand in certain relations to us. This does not prevent us, even in the most local context, from thinking about the world as it is in itself.

I argued in Chapter 1 that a dilemma for the absolute conception of reality, posed by Bernard Williams, can be defused if we are careful to distinguish representations from their content. But his way of putting the dilemma did capture something right about the problem we face in developing our conception of an objective world. Recall the dialectic of Williams's discussion: we have two subjects, A and B, each with some knowledge of the world (perhaps, we might add, in their separate contexts). To understand how each perspective can be a view of the same reality we need to "form a conception of the world which *contains* A and B and their representations," and we need to explain how what each says about the world compares with what the other says. Williams goes on to claim that "indeed, we must be able to form that conception with regard to *every* other representation which might make [a claim to knowledge]." There are two ways to interpret the quantifiers in this last demand. If the claim is that we must form a single conception of the world that incorporates all possible representations of it that might make a claim to knowledge, then I think it is asking for something that could be achieved only if the foundationalist picture were essentially right, and that is asking too much. What we can reasonably demand is that for any representations we might find in the world, if we take them to make correct claims to knowledge, then there will be a way to construct a context in which we can represent their representations as perspectives on the same reality. This is enough to be an ambitious demand, and I think it is enough to ground a robustly realistic conception of the world.

References

Alter, A. and S. Walter (eds.) (2007) *Phenomenal Concepts and Phenomenal Knowledge: New Essays on Consciousness and Physicalism* (Oxford: Oxford University Press).

Auster, P. (1985) *The New York Trilogy* (New York: Penguin Books).

Beaney, M. (1997) *The Frege Reader* (Oxford: Blackwell).

Block, N. (2003) 'Mental Paint', in M. Hahn and B. Ramberg (eds.), *Reflections and Replies: Essays on the Philosophy of Tyler Burge* (Cambridge, Mass.: MIT Press).

Boghossian, P. (1989) 'Content and Self-Knowledge', *Philosophical Topics* **17:** 5–26.

—— (1994) 'The Transparency of Mental Content', *Philosophical Perspectives* **8**: 33–50.

Brown, J. (2004) *Anti-Individualism and Knowledge* (Cambridge, Mass.: MIT Press).

Burge, T. (1988) 'Individualism and Self-Knowledge', *Journal of Philosophy* **85**: 649–63.

—— (1998) 'Memory and Self-Knowledge', in P. Ludlow, and N. Martin (eds.), *Externalism and Self-Knowledge* (Stanford: CSLI Publications), 351–71.

Byrne, A. (2001) 'Intentionalism Defended', *Philosophical Review* **110**: 199–240.

—— (2002) 'Something about Mary', *Grazer Philosophical Studies* **63**: 213–72.

—— and D. Hilbert (eds.) (1997) *Readings on Color 1, The Philosophy of Color* (Cambridge, Mass.: MIT Press).

—— and H. Logue (eds.) (forthcoming) *Disjunctivism: Contemporary Readings* (Cambridge, Mass.: MIT Press).

—— and J. Thomson (eds.) (2007) *Modality and Content* (Oxford: Oxford University Press).

Campbell, J. (1993) 'A Simple View of Colour', in J. Haldane and C. Wright (eds.), *Reality, Representation, and Projection* (Oxford: Oxford University Press). Reprinted in A. Byrne and D. Hilbert (1997), 177–90. Page references to the latter.

Chalmers, D. (2003) 'The Content and Epistemology of Phenomenal Belief', in Q. Smith and A. Jokic (eds.), *Conciousness: New Philosophical Perspectives* (Oxford: Oxford University Press), 220–72.

——(2006). 'Perception and the Fall from Eden', in T. Gendler and J. Hawthorne (eds.), *Perceptual Experience* (Oxford: Oxford University Press).

Crimmins, M. (1992) 'I falsely believe that *p*', *Analysis* **52**: 191.

Davidson, D. (1991) 'Epistemology Externalized', *Dialectica* **45**: 191–202.

Dennett, D. (1978) 'Where Am I?', in *Brainstorms: Philosophical Essays on Mind and Psychology* (Montgomery, Vermont: Bradford Books).

Devitt, M. (1983) 'Realism and the Renegade Putnam: a Critical Study of *Meaning and the Moral Sciences*', *Nous* **17**: 291–301.

Donnellan, K. (1972) 'Names and Identifying Descriptions', in G. Harman and D. Davidson (eds.), *Semantics for Natural Language* (Dordrecht: D. Reidel), 356–79.

Dummett, M. (1978) 'Frege's Distinction between Sense and Reference', in M. Dummett, *Truth and Other Enigmas* (Cambridge, Mass.: Harvard University Press), 116–44.

——(1981) *The Interpretation of Frege's Philosophy* (Cambridge, Mass.: Harvard University Press).

Elga, A. (2000) 'Self-Locating Belief and the Sleeping Beauty Problem', *Analysis* **60**: 143–7.

Evans, G. (1979) 'Reference and Contingency', *The Monist* **62**: 161–89.

Fine, K. (2005) 'Tense and Reality', in K. Fine, *Modality and Tense: Philosophical Papers* (Oxford: Oxford University Press), 261–320.

Frege, G. (1919/1956) 'The Thought: A Logical Inquiry', *Mind* **65**: 287–311.

Garcia-Carpintero, M. and J. Macia (eds.) (2006) *Two-Dimensional Semantics* (Oxford: Oxford University Press).

Hare, C. (2007) 'Self-Bias, Time-Bias, and the Metaphysics of Self and Time', *Journal of Philosophy* **104**: 350–73.

Hawthorne, J. (2004) *Knowledge and Lotteries* (Oxford: Oxford University Press).

—— and T. Szabo Gendler (eds.) (2002) *Conceivability and Possibility* (New York: Oxford University Press).

Heim, I. (1983) 'On the Projection Problem for Presupposition', in M. Barlow and D. Flickinger (eds.), *WCCFL 2: Second Annual West Coast Conference on Formal Linguistics*, 114–25.

Horgan, T. (2004) 'Sleeping Beauty Awakened: New Odds at the Dawn of the New Day', *Analysis* **64**: 10–21.

Hume, D. (1748/1977) *An Enquiry Concerning Human Understanding*, ed. by E. Steinberg (Indianapolis: Hackett Publishing Company).

Jackson, F. (1982) 'Epiphenomenal Qualia', *Philosophical Quarterly* **32**: 127–36.

—— (1998) *From Metaphysics to Ethics: a Defense of Conceptual Analysis* (Oxford: Oxford University Press).

Johnston, M. (1992) 'How to Speak of the Colors', *Philosophical Studies* **68**: 221–63. Reprinted, with postscript, in Byrne and Hilbert (1997), 137–76.

Kripke, S. (1972) *Naming and Necessity* (Cambridge, Mass.: Harvard University Press).

—— (1979) 'A Puzzle about Belief', in A. Margalit (ed.), *Meaning and Use* (Dordrecht: Reidel), 239–83.

—— (1982) *Wittgenstein on Rules and Private Language* (Cambridge, Mass.: Harvard University Press).

Lewis, D. (1979) 'Attitudes de dicto and de se', *Philosophical Review* **88**: 513–43. Reprinted in Lewis (1983). Page references to the latter.

—— (1981) 'What Puzzling Pierre Does not Believe', *Australasian Journal of Philosophy* **59**: 283–9. Reprinted in Lewis (1999), 408–17. Page references to the latter.

—— (1983) *Phlosophical Papers, I* (Oxford: Oxford University Press).

—— (1984) 'Putnam's Paradox', *Australasian Journal of Philosophy* **62**: 221–36. Page references to the latter.

—— (1988) 'What Experience Teaches', *Proceedings of the Russell Society* (University of Sydney), 29–57. Reprinted in Lewis (1999), 262–90. Page references to the latter.

—— (1995) 'Should a Materialist Believe in Qualia?' *Australasian Journal of Philosophy* **73**: 140–4. Reprinted in Lewis (1999), 325–31. Page references to the latter.

—— (1996) 'Elusive Knowledge', *Australasian Journal of Philosophy* **74**: 549–67. Reprinted in Lewis (1999), 418–45. Page references to the latter.

—— (1999) *Papers in Metaphysics and Epistemology* (Cambridge: Cambridge University Press).

—— (2001) 'Sleeping Beauty: a Reply to Elga', *Analysis* **61**: 171–6.

Loar, B. (1990) 'Phenomenal States', *Philosophical Perspectives* **4**: 113–29.

Lodge, D. (2001) *Thinks . . .* (New York: Viking).

McDowell, J. (1977) 'On the Sense and Reference of a Proper Name', *Mind* **86**: 159–85.

Nagel, T. (1986) *The View from Nowhere* (Oxford: Oxford University Press).

Nemirow, L. (1990) 'Physicalism and the cognitive role of acquaintance', in W. Lycan (ed.), *Mind and Cognition: a Reader* (Oxford: Blackwell).

Nida-Rümelin, M. (1995) 'What Mary Couldn't Know: Belief and Phenomenal States', in T. Metzinger (ed.), *Conscious Experience* (Exeter: Imprint Academic), 219–41.

Peacocke, C. (1984) 'Colour Concepts and Colour Experience', *Synthese* **58**: 365–82. Reprinted in A. Byrne and D. Hilbert (eds.), *Readings on Color 1, The Philosophy of Color* (Cambridge, Mass.: MIT Press), 51–65. Page references to the latter.

Perry, J. (1977) 'Frege on Demonstratives', *Philosophical Review* **86**: 474–97. Reprinted in Perry (2000). Page references to the latter.

—— (1979) 'The Problem of the Essential Indexical', *Noûs* **13**: 3–21. Reprinted in Perry (2000).

—— (1999) *Knowledge, Possibility and Consciousness* (Cambridge, Mass.: MIT Press).

—— (2000) *The Problem of the Essential Indexical and Other Essays* (Stanford: CSLI Publications).

Putnam, H. (1977) 'Realism and Reason', *Proceedings of the American Philosophical Association* **50**: 483–98.

Quine, W. V. (1956) 'Quantifiers and Propositional Attitudes', *Journal of Philosophy* **53**: 177–87. Reprinted in Quine, *Ways of Paradox and other Essays* (New York: Random House, 1966), 183–94.

—— (1960) *Word and Object* (Cambridge, Mass.: MIT Press).

Russell, B. (1917/1957) 'Knowledge by Acquaintance and Knowledge by Description', in Russell, *Mysticism and Logic* (New York: Doubleday), 202–24.

Sellars, W. (1956/1997) *Empiricism and the Philosophy of Mind* (Cambridge, Mass.: Harvard University Press).

Simons, D. and R. Rensin (2005) 'Change Blindness: Past, Present, and Future Trends', *Cognitive Sciences* **9**: 16–20.

Stalnaker, R. (1984) *Inquiry* (Cambridge, Mass.: MIT Press).

—— (1988) 'Belief Attribution and Context', in R. Grimm and D. Merrill (eds.), *Contents of Thought* (Tucson: University of Arizona Press), 140–56. Reprinted in Stalnaker (1999), 150–66.

—— (1999) *Context and Content* (Oxford: Oxford University Press).

—— (2001) 'On Considering a Possible World as Actual', *Proceedings of the Aristotelian Society,* supp. vol. **75**: 141–56. Reprinted in Stalnaker (2003c), 188–200.

—— (2002) 'Common Ground', *Linguistics and Philosophy* **25**: 701–21.

—— (2003a) 'Conceptual Truth and Metaphysical Necessity', in Stalnaker (2003c), 201–15.

—— (2003b) 'On Thomas Nagel's Objective Self', in Stalnaker (2004c), 253–75.

—— (2003c) *Ways a World Might Be: Metaphysical and Anti-metaphysical Essays* (Oxford: Oxford University Press).

—— (2004) 'Assertion Revisited: on the interpretation of two-dimensional modal semantics', *Philosophical Studies* **118**: 299–322. Reprinted in Garcia-Carpintero and Macia (2006), 293–309.

—— (2008) 'What is De Re Belief?', in J. Almog and P. Leonardi (eds.), *The Philosophy of David Kaplan* (Oxford: Oxford University Press).

Stoljar, D. (2005) 'Physicalism and Phenomenal Concepts', *Mind and Language* **20**: 469–94.

Sturgeon, S. (1994) 'The Epistemic View of Subjectivity', *Journal of Philosophy* **91**: 221–35.

—— (forthcoming) 'Stalnaker on Sensuous Knowledge', *Philosophical Studies*.

Tye, M. (1988) 'Externalism and Memory', *Proceedings of the Aristotelian Society* **72**: 77–94.

—— (2003) 'A Theory of Phenomenal Concepts', in A. O'Hear (ed.), *Minds and Persons* (Cambridge: Cambridge University Press), 91–103.

Weintraub, R. (2004) 'Sleeping Beauty: a Simple Solution', *Analysis* **64**: 8–10.

Williams, B. (1978) *Descartes: The Project of Pure Enquiry* (New York: Routledge).

Williamson, T. (2001) *Knowledge and Its Limits* (Oxford: Oxford University Press).

Yablo, S. (2006) 'No Fool's Cold: Notes on Illusions of Possibility', in Garcia-Carpintero and Macia (2006), 327–45.

Index